You've Been Lillied

© Ryley Forrester 2009
Published by FRP Liverpool

Paperback
ISBN 978-0-9563256-0-0

Hardback
ISBN 978-0-9563256-1-7

All rights reserved. No part of this publication may be reproduced, stored in a retrieval system, or transmitted in any form or by any means, electronic, mechanical, photocopying, recording or otherwise, without prior permission from the publisher.

Thanks to everyone involved in the making of this book. To all those who gave their photographs, their memories and their time.
Especially to Steven, Francis, Frank Riley and Michael March.

THE LILY CENTRE
Breast Cancer Support Group

93-97 Silvester Street
Liverpool L5 8SF

Telephone / Fax 0151 207 1343 / 9055
Email lilycentre@btopenworld.com

www.lilycentre.org.uk

Registered Charity No. 1087847

Ten Years of The Lily Centre

Ryley Forrester

FRP Liverpool

To Peggy and Winnie

Thanks for giving me the opportunity to put together the words for your story. It has helped to keep me warm during last winter's cold and dark nights. It has also helped those around me, who have needed a positive focus to rely on while they endured the most traumatic time of their lives. So for this, I remain truly grateful. In all of my years in professional writing I have never so much enjoyed the education and inspiration that your magnificent contribution towards emotional wellbeing in this country has provided for me. I have no doubt whatsoever that your durability, courage and strength will rub off on others as the story unfolds. Please accept this small contribution towards your work as a token of my affection.

Ryley Forrester

To Pat
My life, my inspiration.

For Jess
The light of our lives.

Contents

Thank You From Peggy and Winnie ... ... Page 10

Preface ... ... Page 11

Foreword With Dave Hickson ... ... Page 12

Introduction ... ... Page 14

Chapter One
From Small Acorns, Oak Trees Grow ... ... Page 16

Chapter Two
Angels with Scouse Accents ... ... Page 27

Picture Section One
The Lily Centre Photo Album ... ... Page 32

Chapter Three
Love, Hope, Understanding and Inspiration ... ... Page 33

Chapter Four
Peggy ... ... Page 37

Chapter Five
Winnie ... ... Page 43

Chapter Six
Lily ... ... Page 48

Chapter Seven
Teamwork ... ... Page 56

Chapter Eight
The Lily Centre ... ... Page 63

CHAPTER NINE
A SIGHT FOR SORE EYES … … … … … … … … … … … … PAGE 66

CHAPTER TEN
LET THE PEOPLE HAVE THEIR SAY … … … … … … … PAGE 71

PICTURE SECTION ONE
THE LILY CENTRE PHOTO ALBUM … … … … … … … PAGE 80

CHAPTER ELEVEN
COINCIDENCES, OR IS IT MEANT TO BE … … … … … PAGE 86

CHAPTER TWELVE
SPECIAL SPANISH ANGELS. THE HOLY TRINITY … … … PAGE 88

CHAPTER THIRTEEN
MIND OVER MATTER … … … … … … … … … … … … PAGE 90

CHAPTER FOURTEEN
WHEN THE GOING GETS TOUGH … … … … … … … PAGE 95

CHAPTER FIFTEEN
WHO CARES FOR THE CARER? … … … … … … … … PAGE 100

CHAPTER SIXTEEN
LET THE COST OF THE FEW LAY LIGHT ON THE MANY … PAGE 109

CHAPTER SEVENTEEN
COMFORT ON THE WINGS OF A NIGHTINGALE … … … … PAGE 112

LILY OF THE VALLEY … … … … … … … … … … … PAGE 114

WHERE TO FIND THE LILY CENTRE … … … … … … PAGE 116

THANK YOU FROM PEGGY AND WINNIE

We would just like to say a big thank you to all who have helped us to develop The Lily Centre over the years into what it is today.

It would not have been possible without you. You all know who you are and, it is a pity that we couldn't name you in this publication but there are so many wonderful supporters that we are lucky to know, it would have needed a book of its own in order to include everyone.

However there is one person who attracts a big thank you. A very special person who has been with us since our very early days. A person so loyal, so supportive and so special. Such a hard-working and committed lady. That person is Pat Heron, 'our back-bone'. We love you Pat.

As we now progress through our tenth anniversary year there will be plenty of chances for us to hopefully meet up together and enjoy the celebration events which we have got planned. The future of The Lily Centre and indeed, more Lily Centres is very important but we are so proud of the people of Liverpool for what they have helped us to achieve so far.

Where else could it have happened?

God bless you all

Peggy and Winnie

PREFACE

Here lies a story of devastation disaster and depression, following on towards courage, bravery and hope, all brought together by two remarkable women who refused to lie down and die after being stricken with one of the worst possible conditions that a woman has to face.

Their story already provides inspiration for many thousands of people throughout the world and it is in this year of 2009 we live to celebrate the tenth anniversary of the birth of their initiative.

For it was ten years ago this summer when they first met to set up what is now the most successful self supporting breast cancer group in this country and beyond.

Their work already crosses the political, religious, social and racial divides they have no enemies as their contribution is only aimed at the benefit of all mankind.

FOREWORD

WITH DAVE HICKSON

Anyone who had the privilege to watch Dave Hickson play football will testify that here was a unique player who graced the fields of Goodison Park, Anfield and Prenton Park, giving thousands upon thousands of supporters a pleasure which they will never forget.

During the 1950s and 1960s, Dave won the heart of fans with his dashing displays at centre forward for Everton, Liverpool and Tranmere Rovers.

Fearless in all he did Dave Hickson, with his ability and passion would terrorise opposing defences up and down the length and breadth of the country. It did not matter how big or tough they were because Dave Hickson's bravery knew no bounds, he could mix it with the best of them.

Dave was the real life Roy of the Rovers of his day and every young lad on Merseyside found inspiration from such a splendid ambassador for the game of football. That is why I am so proud for Dave to agree to contribute his comments towards the foreword of this book.

"I played my last charity game for the over the hill mob when I was seventy seven years old", Dave tells.

Would you believe that? Seventy seven years old and he still had his quiff. Maybe by the time he is ninety, he will just settle for a game of five a side.

Now that he has hung up his boots it does not mean that his contributions to charity have become any less. In fact as well as his job at Everton, Dave is still very much in demand.

Dave explained, "My wife, Pat and I have been patrons and supporters of The Lily Centre for about seven or eight years now, and we are both looking forward to this years celebrations of the centres tenth anniversary.

We would both like to express our admiration for these two remarkable women, in the work that they have done in the past and also for the work which they will continue to do in the future.

Pat and I appreciate the benefits which Peggy and Winnie have brought into place so that those people who need a place to go can share their thoughts with others in a similar position.

We will always try our best to support and attend any fund raising events or charity nights which are arranged, as we take great pleasure in helping to sustain these women within the work that they do.

We both look forward to the publication of the book and hope it will help to promote, for years to come this truly magnificent cause".

Yours truly
Dave Hickson

INTRODUCTION

CHARITY BEGINS AT HOME

So that the reader may gain a useful overview from an early stage of what this publication is all about an attempt has been made to provide a brief illustration of the historical, geographical and social issues prevailing at the time which greatly affected the lives of those concerned.

1949 – 2009

In the summer of 1949, two proud fathers celebrated the births of two baby girls, born into their respective families. As it happens, these two dads were school colleagues, born within twenty four hours of each other and both attending Saint Silvester's School, just West of Scotland Road.

The Second World War clean up was at its height when twenty eight year old Jim and Winnie Walsh, proclaimed their daughters introduction to this planet, as 'Little Winnie' first saw the light of day.

As these celebrations for Winnie's birth were taking place, Peter and Mary Innes, were also delighted to announce the birth of their little baby girl, 'Peggy'. This had taken place just around the corner a few days earlier.

Given the close connections of their fathers, the close proximity of their births and the closeness of their birthdays it seemed inevitable that these two kids would eventually meet up. They would go on to live and work within the same area, go to school, go to work, get married, have their own kids, just as most girls do, and continue to live in the same district for most of their lives.

The amazing fact is that they never actually met until 1999. After both had contracted breast cancer, and both were determined to look at ways to beat the disease. And it was that first meeting of a yet to be organised, self-help group where Peggy and Winnie became inseparable. Within their commitment and determination to build up an initiative which would go on to help thousands of women from far and wide in their attempt to cope with such a critical illness.

So it was against this historical backdrop, of war, calamity, demolition and destruction, amidst the people of Scotland Road; an inner city area already blighted by poverty and poor housing where Peggy O'Brien and Winnie Keating began to create this extraordinary success in providing those in need with the moral and spiritual support, which is so vital for recovery.

It was, these two women who took on themselves, the care and support of, by this time, frail, but still holding a remarkable sense of humour, Lily Halligan, as one of their first members of the self-help group.

From these humble beginnings would develop a new unique approach to care work that had not been known in this country before. Yes, it was these two woman whose courage, hard work and passion over the last ten years has created a phenomenon which is now recognised, appreciated and applauded by the highest in the land.

It is held up as a way forward in the emotional and morale boosting care of patients who have to travel through such an awful time in their lives.

The following pages attempt to provide the reader with an accurate picture and therefore a fair understanding of the magnificent contribution towards the important benefits, now enjoyed by so many, all because of the work carried out by Peggy O'Brien and Winnie Keating.

CHAPTER ONE

FROM SMALL ACORNS, OAK TREES GROW

We are now entering into a period of celebrations where many thousands of families will show their thanksgiving on a global basis for the assistance and support that they have received from The Lily Centre during their hours of need.

It will be a time for reflection, a time for joyous recollection of their own stories, which they will enjoy telling to their own kids and grandkids about how they became involved with The Lily Centre and how they now feel so much better because of that involvement.

They will explain to their families about a new feeling of confidence and strength that fulfilled them after they had met Peggy and Winnie.

They will go on to explain to all who are close around them, why it is so important that we preserve and sustain the work of Peggy O'Brien and Winnie Keating so that others in the future who find themselves in a similar position can go on to benefit from the magnificent care and support which their loved ones received in the past.

Many others will choose to remember the hundreds of wonderful events that have been arranged and organised over the last ten years which have helped to galvanise the spirit and keep people together when they needed each other most.

There will also be the healthy amongst us who just want to sit back and marvel at the effect this wondrous place has had upon us, once we become 'Lillied'.

The near and the dear ones, the young and the old,

strangers in the street have all been brought together by this immaculate conception born out of the passion, determination and sheer grit of these two remarkable women who have never taken no for an answer. Their original initiative may sound simple enough on paper but actually putting it into practise becomes a completely different story.

The creation of this self-help group and then The Lily Centre in the beginning took such a massive amount of commitment, drive and durability to establish, that even the healthiest of us would no doubt fail at the first fence. They didn't. It is still difficult to imagine the mammoth physical, emotional and financial struggles which they had to endure while attempting to get the group off the ground as it was blood, sweat and tears that waited to greet them at the outset of this epic journey.

Those humble beginnings saw close family and friends giving what they could in time, finance and emotional support to Peggy and Winnie as they strived on in developing the group.

Difficult lessons were learned during those early days about the economics of this type of work and the constraints in what can be achieved with the resources available. But maybe sometimes things happen for a reason.

Now the group applies substantial bookkeeping skills and good housekeeping methods enabling The Lily Centre to flourish into what it is today.

Every penny received in donations is carefully spent in the appropriate manner so that the giver can be assured that their contribution goes exactly where they want it to go.

There are no figureheads here. Nobody gets anything for nothing and everyone involved is prepared to give up their free time gladly. Yes, even difficult lessons have their place. When all you ever had to start with was a book of stamps to put in your filing cabinet, it tends to teach you prudence as well as appreciating good budget practise.

After begging and scraping around, gathering bits and pieces from all who were prepared to give, whilst at the same time attempting to get the message across to those who may wish to listen, the group began to expand a little.

There had been what may be classed as a 'turning point' in their aspirations when they decided to put on a charity night for other breast cancer sufferers at the New Millennium Centre which was located close by, just off Scotland Road.

There was no place for faint hearts in those days as the group battled for recognition in what it was attempting to achieve. It was only the sheer dedication of both Peggy and Winnie which had enabled the project to develop as far as it had. So it was no easy task to take on the responsibility of arranging and organising a charity event of this type within the local community. But this they did! From these two women there would be no surrender.

As it turned out the night was a huge success. Over £3,000 was raised in what was a full house, over the course of the evening. This money would later be donated to The Royal Liverpool Hospital's breast cancer unit.

Just as important was the newly gained knowledge that local people were now clearly behind them, thus assuring the group that all their efforts were so greatly appreciated.

This early local endorsement would go on to play its part in providing a boost for their spirits as they worked tirelessly in laying the foundation stones that would underpin the development of the project. It could be said that without even realising it at the time they had managed to get the whole neighbourhood 'Lillied'.

Being 'Lillied' of course was a term which would gather momentum as Peggy and Winnie decided to name their newly found premises after the oldest member of their group, Lily Halligan.

It is now often fondly used to describe how someone feels once captured and drawn towards this aura that is transmitted on meeting Peggy and Winnie and the following desire to become useful to the cause thereafter.

The group had spent their formative months using facilities in local meeting rooms which were hardly ideal for what they wanted to achieve and lacked the necessary atmosphere which was needed to instil confidence amongst others.

So Peggy and Winnie were overjoyed when they were able to move on from the Vauxhall Health Centre and the Rotunda Club into their new base in Silvester Street just off Scotland Road.

Their own personalities could now be stamped upon the recently refurbished accommodation which would prove to have a massive effect upon the work and quality of the service that they were aiming to provide.

Little did they realise then just how massive and important this work and this service would turn out to be.

Little could they have known then just how widespread their message and their deeds would become as year by year they captivated the hearts and minds of so many people from all walks of life.

Yes it was here then, on that memorable day, all those years ago when they received the keys to their new centre of operations they were able to take their voluntary services to a new level, working out of The Lily Centre.

Here was a place which would provide the pair with an opportunity to create their own unique atmosphere, in an environment of their own choice; a place where they could make a home from home for the many thousands of people who would eventually cross their threshold.

Peggy and Winnie were now in a position to broaden their horizons, they could now help even more of those affected by this condition to adjust and come to terms with the situation.

This, of course would mean even more work for them but these two women were up for the challenge.

They would recruit more volunteers to augment the support of their close family and friends so that there would be available cover to maintain an already superb quality of service.

Not just anybody would be invited to help. Peggy and Winnie were very aware that their service needed committed and genuine folk to take it forward so they were very cautious and selective in whom they chose to become 'Lillied'.

As the years passed by The Lily Centre and its message of hope began to flourish as more and more people got 'Lillied' then went on to spread the word to others.

Already now well established within its local community, others from further afield began to notice that 'something special' was starting to happen down Scotland Road way.

People across the city were now becoming more interested in this free after care service because there had never been anything quite like it before.

Everyone who visited the centre seemed to get 'Lillied', this strange feeling of being overwhelmed and thrilled at the same time had no bounds. It didn't matter where you came from or who you were it was the same for everybody.

Of course, Peggy and Winnie just got on with it, if the truth was known. It is likely that they didn't notice the fuss that was developing around them as they were too busy working their socks off. Nevertheless more and more of Liverpool's population were becoming so impressed with their contribution towards such a crucial area of healthcare, that a well deserved recognition process began to develop, especially once their message started to cross National and International boundaries.

As the years rolled on it became apparent that this phenomenon from its birthplace in Scotland Road was beginning to gain national momentum. That early vote of confidence and support from the local community was now reaching the ears of others in high office.

People from all over the country were turning their attention to the stories of hope and inspiration being told by many who had been fortunate enough to be touched by The Lily Centre's special surroundings.

A groundswell of awareness emerged as more and more people came out and went public with their feelings.

Superstars of sport and entertainment, top politicians, media experts and even The Royal Family were happy to endorse this wonderful initiative, born from the blood, sweat and tears of these two ordinary women.

This level of recognition, so hard to earn, so long in years to obtain, so richly deserved can now go on to create scope for the development of wider care and attention provided by more Peggys and Winnies throughout the world.

The two women were far too busy to be bothered about others talking about them so when they were nominated for their first top award they thought that the invitation to go along was just to make the numbers up. But it wasn't! They won it!

When they were invited to the final stages of 'Women Making a Difference Award' at Liverpool Town Hall in 2003, they truly believed that it was just a night out where they could perhaps learn from others in how to improve their services.

Little could they have guessed that they would be called to centre stage and then receive the winner's award presented by Cherie Booth. They were totally taken aback with what was going on around them.

Although this success was difficult for them to evaluate at the time it would go on to form the platform for further achievements which would play an important part in bringing their message into the public arena.

This was a first tentative step along the journey from local, then national, and then on to international recognition that we now celebrate today.

The word was now out. Peggy and Winnie had created not just a practical way forward in the aftercare of people suffering from breast cancer but also a new philosophy where anyone needing assurance and emotional support could benefit from their methods.

As if to show that the initial award was no flash in the pan, they went on to win a Merseyside Women of the Year Award the following year at Liverpool's Crown Plaza Hotel. Again they believed that they were there just to make the numbers up as there were so many nominations. But Peggy and Winnie were soon to become surprised and delighted when Cherie Booth appeared from nowhere to announce that they were amongst the winners.

The women went on to enjoy an emotional reunion with Cherie and the tears flowed freely as the impact of this success began to sink in.

For Cherie Booth it was a chance to display her great admiration for the work of these women and to promote the benefits of what it's like to be 'Lillied'.

Cherie Booth was so enthralled by their work that she became a patron and has remained so ever since.

She will often drop into The Lily Centre for a cup of tea and a chat when she is in Liverpool after initially wondering why she had not been invited before.

At first Peggy and Winnie thought that Cherie was a patron in name only. Not a bit of it. She later even arranged for Tim Grestby to organise a flight to London so that they could have a cup of tea and a chat at number 10 Downing Street.

So that little acorn planted in hope so many years ago began to gain strength as those with influence became more aware of its potential use in the well being and care of breast cancer sufferers.

This young oak tree could now spread its branches across the many new milestones it would have to reach as it continued its journey.

Highlights of the journey so far

1999
First ever meeting of the women's self-help group at the Vauxhall Health Centre.

2000
They are given the keys to The Lily Centre and celebrate its official opening.

2001
They open The Lily Centre Garden of Remembrance.

2003
Women Making a Difference Award.

2004
Merseyside Women of the Year Award.

2005
Visit to 10 Downing Street for a cup of tea.

2006
Royal visit to The Lily Centre by The Duchess of Gloucester.

2006
Visit to Buckingham Palace to see the Queen.

2008
Radio City Local Heroes Award.

2009
10th Anniversary Celebrations.

Awards like the ones mentioned don't get handed out for nothing, they reflect year upon year of building a service and its supporting facilities which is second to none.

So, what makes The Lily Centre so different from other self-help groups?

Well, it is truly amazing when you look at the vast amounts of benefits open to anyone who asks for them under one roof.

As well as the obvious emotional and physical support available, together with the superb social network in place, the centre also offers members the use of a gym to keep fit, after which they can have their hair done with the beautician and hairdresser on hand to make them feel and look their best.

Line dancing classes are always well attended and with Reiki, Reflexology, hot stones and Homeopathy keeping members occupied, there is always plenty going on at the centre, to keep everyone in a positive mood.

All of these activities including the day trips to the seaside, weekends away and the fantastic nights out together; arranged by Peggy and Winnie, help to create this informal, unique atmosphere that is enjoyed by all who attend.

A
All Souls
Winnie's School

N
Newz Bar
The major patrons

G
St. Gerard's
Peggy's school

E
Eldon Street
Peggy's first home

L
Limekiln Lane
Winnie & Peggy's Health Centre

S
Slade Street
Winnie's first home

CHAPTER TWO

ANGELS WITH SCOUSE ACCENTS

Many of the acts of goodness and wholesome behaviour go unnoticed today without the slightest recognition from most of us. Maybe it's because the efforts of the people who carry them out can not be sensationalised enough, to jack up the sales of some national newspapers. Perhaps it's not cool to broadcast these magnificent efforts together with the free time given gladly by so many unsung heroes working within the voluntary services on a regular basis.

Even the media tends to focus its hourly news bulletins upon war, rape, murder, road traffic accidents and drug trafficking before it allows any airtime to the tremendous devotion and major contribution made within the activities of ordinary people, all working away for nothing more than the satisfaction of improving the lives of those around them.

Most people live out the majority of their adult lives doing the best they can for their families and friends and this culture helps to build stable and sound communities. Some do a lot of good things while others may be inclined to be a bit selfish so just look after themselves.

Also there are those amongst us who will have the great fortune to be able to jog along life's path without a care in the world. And then there are those who may stumble along the way, who through no fault of their own have to struggle in the face of adversity. Then, set apart from the mere mortals most of us who are subject to normal human behaviour are the chosen few.

The Chosen Few

Well who are the chosen few? They don't look any different from you or me; they have families, responsibilities and human failings just like the rest of us. But they are different.

These are the people who regardless of their own difficulties and negative happenings within their own lives are able to radiate a spirit and transmit a genuine feeling for hope, a real reason for living and a positive attitude towards adversity amongst the community living around them.

They do not crave celebrity status or fame; they are not interested in fortune. They work quietly and effectively amongst their own to dedicate their lives and their utter devotion towards those who have suffered from a similar misfortune as they have themselves.

Perhaps it is because they have come through their own personal traumatic or negative experience that they are so able and qualified to be successful in the provision of understanding and loving hospitality towards others who find themselves in a likewise situation.

To possess a calling for helping the ailing and the sick is in itself a splendid quality to have, but to have to combat and overcome an illness and then go on to find the strength, durability and character that produces comfort and inspiration for so many others can only be described as miraculous.

A God Given Gift

This gift that god has bestowed upon our earth-angels who have been selected, the ability to radiate a spiritual strength amongst all who are fortunate enough to meet them brings out the best in people, who perhaps before were feeling lonely and insecure. This is the gift that makes them different from the rest of us. It makes them unique but God's gift does not come without cost.

Our angels have been there, seen it, done it and got the T shirt. They do know what they are talking about. So it is those particular earth-angels we want to focus on.

Doctors, Nurses and support staff all play an immense role in the care of the sick and the importance of their work should be recognised by everyone, it can not be underestimated. Yet the chosen few stand out even amongst those laudable professionals.

Without our earth-angels who so willingly provide comfort and care at no cost the government would be landed with a massive bill in healthcare, running into millions of pounds. This would eventually fall at the feet of the British taxpayer and that is a fact.

On that basis it can clearly be seen that we all owe a mammoth debt to our angels who so quietly and passively go about their work with the minimum of fuss and without any overall recognition by the nation.

What a shame!

It has to be shameful to be so complacent and to take for granted this major work and contribution put in by the chosen few. In the cold light of day we hardly give them a moment of thought. Sometimes it takes a shock, an unforeseen happening, and a life changing experience for us to eventually realise that these angels exist. Once these earth-angels become apparent however, a whole new world can open up the mind. A genuine sense of humanity and appreciation can take place, leading to a wish or even a need for further education regarding their work and their worth.

Further on comes the desire to play some small part in the process, to find some way of contributing towards sustaining them in what they do.

For those who now see them a whole new outlook on life can develop, where the material world begins to flounder in the sense of importance, worldly priorities change and tolerance levels improve and their presence generates a will to do better.

Being aware of their existence and the work they do helps the mind to become healthier where a new growing up process develops. Greed and avarice diminish leaving the body energised for participation in more wholesome projects.

These are the effects that our angels can generate And guess what? This spiritual level of stimulation and inspiration costs nothing! For this there is no charge!

Our angels are already quite well known to many thousands of scousers throughout the city and indeed to people living in all parts of the world, who remain eternally thankful. Their work and news of their work has already crossed national and international boundaries.

The highest in the land already flock to their workplace so that they can take part in the 'Scouse Message' which our earth's angels deliver. International superstars in the world of sport and entertainment regularly express their own humility and pleasure with being associated with these angels who have an accent 'so exceedingly rare'.

So it's not just me, is it?

It is our own earth's angels with broad Scouse accents who have created the template for the rest of the world to copy. As they continue with their daily tasks of ensuring comfort, confidence and well being amongst the ones they look after.

Meanwhile their charismatic nature and pleasant disposition continues to attract people from all walks of life towards them. For apart from the obvious benefits that are enjoyed by everyone who comes into contact there is something else about meeting them and being in their company.

'Something Abstract'

'Something Spiritual'

'Something Special'

This extraordinary gift which they possess crosses the political, religious and class divides. Nobody, regardless of who they are, what they believe in or what they stand for has ever been turned away from their door and provided that that person who seeks assistance are genuine in their needs and wants, that will always remain the case.

God give me strength

What has to be truly amazing about our earth's angels is not just the comfort and confidence that they generate but also on top of that is this incredible god given talent to be able to bring a new lease of life to so many who, let's face it, in their situation have every right to feel miserable.

Shades of Lazarus spring to mind

"Pick up your bed and walk." So said Jesus Christ when he was healing the sick some 2000 years ago. And just like Jesus with his apostles there was no easy ride for our angels. They would have to face the challenge which was to set in order to reach the position they are today. They would have to fight, scramble and persevere with tremendous mental and physical tests to earn the valued recognition which they now so richly deserve.

The phenomenon which they have created is so unique and simple that it seems that all the great minds in the world could have easily put this together. But they didn't. It was left to Liverpool's own earth's angels to take on the task.

Two ordinary women living their lives amidst their

own communities deep in the heart of Liverpool's inner city. For it was their message which they have been delivering to us all over the past ten years that has finally sunk in and made the rest of the world sit up and begin to recognise the value of this wonderful initiative.

Yes, it was their message, so simple, so straightforward, so honest and so genuine. Easily understood with no strings attached which has such a positive effect on so many thousands of people over the years and still continues to do so today:

'Welcome'

'The kettles always on'

'Make yourself at home'.

The Lily Centre Photo Album

Peggy, Estelle Condliff and Winnie on our first benefit night at the Silvestrian Club, October 1999.

Lily Halligan at the opening of the Lily Centre, August 2000.

Lily's birthday, 4 August 2000.

Lily recieving accolade from Arriva for *Charity of the Year*.

The opening of the Lily Garden, August 2001. After storm clouds in the morning the sun came out to shine brightly all day long.

Peggy, Anne Robinson, Lily and Winnie at Walton Hospital, Friday 19 January 2001.

Lily and Jack Spriggs at the Lord Mayor's Parade.

Peggy and Winnie recieving a cheque from Jack Spriggs when he was Lord Mayor.

Estelle and Pat Condliff with Peggy and Winnie, 2003.

Winnie, Dominique and Peggy, 2003, in The Lily Centre office.

Winnie and Tommy Keating.

Lily with Dr Helen McKendrick at the Christmas Raffle.

Lily, Peggy and Winnie at Walton Hospital.

Our first meeting with Cherie Booth QC at the *Merseyside Women Making a Difference* awards, at Liverpool Town Hall, 2003.

Lily with the bike-riders, July 2003.

Peggy and Winnie with Duncan McKenzie and Alan Ball, when Alan became patron, 2004.

Arriving at 10 Downing Street for lunch with Cherie Booth QC, November 2004.

Winnie and Peggy with Sue Geddes, (Cherie Booth's PR lady) and Pat Heron, 2004.

Steve Riley, 2004.

Emma Phillips with Winnie and Peggy, 2003.

The Lily Centre football team and they can play a bit as well.

Dean Sullivan, Sara White, Eithne Brown and Pauline Fleming, September 2006.

Peggy with Alan Hansen, 2006.

Roger Philips, Angela O'Connor, Marina Dalglish, Norma Meridith, Sandy Andrews, and in the front row, Peggy, Winnie and Pauline Daniels, 2006.

Maureen Fitzpatrick, Cherie Booth, May Quinn, Tony McGann and Estelle Condliff.

Pat, Peggy, Cherie and Winnie.

Cherie meets the menfolk.

One of Cherie's many visits.

Steve Riley, Alec Parks, Les Allen, Tommy Keating and Peter O'Brien.

Cherie Booth and Sue Lee from the *Liverpool Echo* with members of the Lily Centre.

Peggy, Alec Parks and Winnie, 2003.

Dave Hickson and Pat. Dave is still looking for a game of five-a-side.

Dave Watson with Peggy, May 2007.

At Buckingham Palace.

Mary Richards with Peggy and Winnie.

Jimmy and Ann King with Jen Heyes.

Dean Sullivan and Rachel Cain at a benefit night at the Eldonian, October 2007.

Pauline and Paul at the Eldonian Christmas Party, 2005.

Lily members with the Lord Mayor and Lady Mayoress, Paul and Hillary Clarke.

Winnie, Roger Phillips and Peggy at Liverpool Town Hall, 2004.

CHAPTER THREE

LOVE, HOPE, UNDERSTANDING AND INSPIRATION

Throughout the ages, the city of Liverpool has produced its fair share of children who aspire to preach love, hope, understanding and inspiration for the rest of the world to follow. This message has been strong and important when applied to national and international affairs and attitudes.

We have only to look at the contributions made by Lennon, McCartney, Harrison and Starr to get a feel for the effect that Liverpool's message can have upon the rest of the planet.

So, the Liverpool born preachers are already an integral part of history, and rightly so, for the words that they spread love and happiness all over the globe.

What about those who actually practised 'love, hope, understanding and inspiration'. Those whose instinct it was to live their lives in such a way that it gave the poets and the minstrels the material to work upon, in order to produce their words and songs which would go on to captivate the world. Those who were born with the 'God given gift' of being able to quietly inspire all around them without fame or fortune and most certainly without fuss without even realising it?

These are the people that this publication will focus upon. People whose actions rather than words, produced the foundations for preachers, church leaders, musicians and politicians to be able to build their celebrations of Liverpool life upon. These are the 'Real People'.

'Blessed are the meek, for they will one day inherit paradise'.

Someone once said that the greatest gift that can be bestowed upon one by another is 'time'. The time to understand, the time to build some hope, the time it takes to show love, the time to share. Once this time is given and received the inspiration begins.

Here in this book on the following pages is the story of those people who have been blessed by their god with the ability and strength to act out and devote their lives on earth to the wellbeing and healthcare of others.

There's a Place

There's a place where you can go

If you feel low

If you're alone

You can share a space with those who know
just how you feel.

You're not on your own.

All your troubles and sorrows
don't have to end up in tears.

For, they can show you tomorrows
which can last for years.

So there's a place where you can go.

It just needs you to make it so.

Peggy

It only takes a little spark
to make a flame burn so brightly.
But only God can plant that spark
in those in which he chooses.
And the ones most able to carry the light
are the ones in which he uses.

CHAPTER FOUR

PEGGY

Peggy O'Brien had just greeted the visitor to her home with the usual warm and friendly welcome. It was during the onset of summer in 1999 when a local nurse called on Peggy to see how she was getting along after undergoing a major operation to combat breast cancer just over a year ago.

She was still coming to terms with the situation in which she found herself, as the impact had turned her life and the lives of her family upside down.

Being told that you are suffering from cancer can be the ultimate traumatic experience for any human being and Peggy had needed time to digest and reflect upon this devastating information over the last twelve months or so.

But Peggy was made out of strong stuff. She had already seen a lot of life and was well aware of the ups and downs most of us have to go though.

She was just not the type to take this sort of blow on the chin and her natural personality would not allow doom and gloom to set in. Peggy was well equipped for a battle.

So as the conversation between the two women revolved around Peggy's general health and well being the local nurse mentioned the prospect of starting up a self-help group which could be developed amongst the local people in the area who had found themselves in similar circumstances.

The nurse asked Peggy, "Would you be interested in starting such a group?" Peggy's response was immediate: "Yes, Okay! Why not! Let's do it!"

Peggy later explains, "I saw this as an opportunity to give a little bit back for the care that I had received so far".

And so it followed. A date was set for the first meeting of the self-help group to be held on 7 June 1999 at 2:00pm until 4:00pm.

No one could have predicted just how important this date would become to the outcome and shape of future events as history now informs us.

"I remember getting there on time and was just sitting down to have a chat with the others who were there when Winnie popped her head in, it was the first time that we had met. There were only five of us in total when we all sat down ready to begin. It was very informal at first, as you can imagine as this was the first time we had come together in this way the conversation was quite general until we all broke the ice. Winnie and I just seemed to click straight away. I immediately felt that I knew what she was going to say next and she later told me that she had felt the same. Telepathic or what! As our small group gradually gained confidence with each other and so became more able to talk about themselves and the project it became obvious to us that just two hours were not going to be enough time to give, if we were going to make something of it.".

Little could any of them have imagined at that time just how successful this project would eventually become?

Peggy goes on: "The group became a little bit bigger as we went along and we examined things we might be able to do to help others in a practical way who were facing the same problems as we faced. We decided to put on a fund raising event to be held at The New Millennium Centre where we aimed to raise money which would go towards the breast cancer unit at Liverpool's Royal Teaching Hospital.

Our group had grown in size so we had a few more people who were willing to muck in and help out which meant that we could put on an event of a decent size. We were all surprised and delighted when we saw the amount of people who came through the doors that night. It seemed that the whole area had flocked to the event, so much so, the bar ran out of ale at one point and they had to send out for emergency supplies in order to cope with the demand.

We raised three thousand pounds that night! Doctor Chris Holcombe and his family together with some of the breast care nurses also attended that evening and they were all delighted to learn that the money raised would go towards obtaining equipment for the treatment of breast cancer. The success of that night gave our confidence a major boost and it also drew some much needed attention as to what we were trying to achieve.

But, we knew that if we were to go further, then our present meeting venues such as the Vauxhall Health Centre and the Rotunda Club would not be sufficient for our needs. What could we do to ensure that the group stayed together and even increase its numbers? This was the problem which we were now facing.

That's why I bless the day when I first met Paul Flanagan. We needed somewhere warm and friendly to create the atmosphere of an ordinary living room in an ordinary house, which we felt would be more inviting and attractive to people who at that time would be at a very low ebb."

Peggy and Winnie were very grateful to the surgery for allowing them to use the facilities at the Vauxhall Health Centre but they had quickly realised that the more time spent in developing the group, the better the service would be. So if they were to move on, they would need their own place.

"Maybe the council could help, it was worth a try. The housing office was based just up the road in Cramner Street, so I went along there to see if there were any empty properties they had, perhaps somewhere where the council found was hard to let would do?

Mike McDonald, the Housing Officer with whom I spoke, was very sympathetic but unfortunately he had to work within the constraints and rules of the council and there were no provisions for such a request to be granted. However, he said, bear with me because I think I know a man who might be able to help you. And that's how we first met Paul Flanagan.

After the initial introductions he took me around the corner in his car to a three story block of flats in Woodstock Street, just off Scotland Road, facing St. Anthony's Church.

Paul's company were busy refurbishing the block to a very high standard and he proceeded to open the door to a ground floor flat located very close to the entrance gates, which at the time was being used to store materials.

'Look', he said, 'This is for you if you want it. For as long as you like. Rent free'.

Oh my god, I thought, trying not to pinch myself, do we want it, a ground floor, whole flat, no stairs, hot and cold water, heat and light, already installed? You bet we wanted it!

I must confess it was difficult to hold back my joy. I was in fact flabbergasted. For here was a man with kids himself to bring up, (I had noticed the twin baby seats in his car), giving us a whole ground floor flat, located right in the centre of our activities with easy access to buses and trains as well as being close to the city centre. What more could we ask for?

When I got home I rang Winnie to tell her the news.

'You're not going to believe this Winnie, but I've just

met a fellah called Paul Flanagan and he has given us the use of a complete flat in Woodstock Street, for as long as we want it'.

Winnie became as excited as I was, while we chatted away happily about how this was going to improve the things we were trying to do, and how our contribution to people who had suffered like ourselves could now become greater.

All this from a man we didn't know from Adam!

We decided at this stage not to say anything to anyone. I suppose then, that we were still wondering if it were true.

Week by week, over the next few months we would go along to the flat just to see how work was progressing.

By the time we had reached October, the month of our first fundraising night, we had plucked up enough courage and confidence to declare to everyone that we now had our own premises.

As the flat entered into its later stages of refurbishment, Winnie and I would keep up our visits, putting our plans together for how we would like things to turn out.

One day, we were busy chatting away about paint for the ceilings and walls, we thought it would be cheaper to just buy white paint and use dyes to colour it, rather than pay for the more expensive pastel shades.

One of the lads who worked for Flanagan's overheard our conversation and he asked us: 'What colours do you want?'

We told him what we were hoping to do and that we would buy the paint between us. The next time we called, the work was all done in the colours we wanted. No charge! We just could not believe our luck".

Winnie

A gift God-given a gift so rare.
A reason to love and a reason to care.
To work so hard for the benefit of all.
Never to complain about God's call.

CHAPTER FIVE

WINNIE

As Winnie collected the morning post from the hallway on that fateful day in the spring of 1999, her mind was occupied by other things. Still adjusting to the recent loss of her Mother and loving Grandmother to her own children, she was still facing up to the challenge of keeping everyone's spirits up despite the fact that her own health had seen better days.

Diagnosed with breast cancer some three years earlier Winnie Keating had to face the harsh reality of life, when things go wrong. Sometimes it seemed that there was a mountain to climb.

This devastating challenge of facing up to her health problems, while, at the same time keeping the family together was not exactly a challenge to relish.

Like it or not, the challenge was there and Winnie would soon go on to gain the strength to meet it and beat it head on.

She sat down at the breakfast table and began to open the post. The usual stuff was there; bills, special offers, advertisements and amongst all this was a letter from the Health Centre in Limekiln Lane.

They were asking if she was interested in forming a self-help group for women suffering from breast cancer. At first sight she wasn't sure. Did she want to get involved? At that point in time her confidence wasn't at its highest and anyway what could she offer in her state of health right now? Would there be enough people turning up to make it work? Where would any outside support come from?

All of these questions crossed Winnie's mind as she considered the idea; after thinking this over for a while and after a brief discussion with her husband Tommy, who was totally supportive in all that she did.

Winnie decided not to bother going along at first. Then, a short time later she received a telephone call from the district nurse based at the Health Centre. The nurse was following up the earlier letter and asking to see if Winnie would like to attend an initial meeting of the self-help group which was going to be held at the Health Centre on 7th June 1999. On being asked the question Winnie immediately changed her mind and replied: "Yes, okay. I will come along".

As she agreed to the invitation Winnie could never have realised that the date of this first meeting would prove to play such a prominent part in future events. Some may call it coincidence, but there are many others who would suggest that: It was meant to be.

It was on this day, 7th June 1999 that Winnie Keating first met Peggy O'Brien at a venue which was to provide the early stepping stones for a relationship between two souls who would go on to form an amazing partnership that would stand the test of time for years and years to come.

So much so that this unique coming together of hearts and minds has developed into an initiative over the last ten years which has already become legendary in the folklore and history books of the City of Liverpool.

"We hit it off right away", says Winnie. "And as we got to know each other, talking about the things women talk about we realised how much together we had in common. Although there were only a few of us to start off with we got enough from each other to look forward to the next meeting when the attendance doubled to ten people. I think it was at this stage that we decided that more time and better facilities were needed if the project was to be a success."

That decision was to prove to be the turning point in propelling the initiative through time into what it has turned out to be today.

Winnie's relationship with Peggy began to blossom even further when they discovered that their Father's Jim and Peter went to the same school together and were actually born within twenty four hours of each other.

On top of that they soon realised that they themselves were the same age, being born within a week of each other in the same year and within a short walking distance of each other.

Truly amazing!

"It just made us realise how alike we were and that we both wanted the same things; to be able enough to focus on what we were attempting to do. As well as having a laugh and a joke along the way, after all laughter does you good, doesn't it?

I admired Peggy for her tenacity, her positive attitude; always willing to have a go, no matter what the odds. We would spend many a long hour in those days deep in conversations about where we wanted to go and where we would like to be as the weeks passed by."

Even at this early point some onlookers were noticing that Winnie and Peggy were beginning to become inseparable, 'Joined at the hip', so to speak. They were doing everything together and remained totally focused on their objectives.

"Lily Halligan was one of our earlier members and the senior to all of us. She was in her eighties at the time and her stories of life in the war, as well as the hilarious things which she got up to in her youth would keep us spell bounded and uplifted during some of the earlier difficult times.

That's why we both decided to name the centre after her, as a little tribute to the way she had responded to our care and attention.

Lily would want us to remain cheerful and to keep everyone's spirits up and that's what we have attempted to do. It seems to work for us.

A good laugh and a joke certainly helps your emotional state as well as your physical condition, and we do both, often. Lily loved a good laugh and so do we.

Peggy and I always say that it was a pity we didn't contract the condition earlier, because if that was the case, we could have helped so many other people who had found themselves in our situation".

CHAPTER SIX

LILY

It was on the 4th August 1915 that little Lily Halligan first saw the light of day. This small bundle of joy was born to Joe and Pearl Halligan, who at the time were living in the tough working class district of Everton, a few miles North of Liverpool City Centre.

The timing of Lily's birth could not have been worse. It came at the onset of the worst episode in history of man's inhumanity to man. The First World War was now underway and this meant thousands upon thousands of people would eventually lose their lives. Consequently this would be recorded in history as the beginning of the worst ever man made disaster the planet had ever known.

"It will be over by Christmas", proclaimed the politicians, yet four years later, the death toll was rising into millions and this was only the beginning.

The Second World War had yet to come. Such was the conflict and brutality that every village, town or city in Britain would be affected in some way or another. Europe would be devastated by death and destruction as more and more nations became involved in the hostilities and unrest.

For the people of Liverpool the situation was even worse. Being then, the most important seaport in the country with seven miles of docklands the city was vital to the war effort as well as being home to large parts of the Royal and Merchant navies. Liverpool's links with transatlantic trade also made it a prime target for enemy attack for many years to come.

So this is the backdrop for kids in their formative years, hoping to grow up and prosper within their native city. To say the outlook looked bleak would be an understatement.

However, that was the reality that had to be faced so most ordinary folk would have no choice but to try and live life as normally as was possible given the circumstances.

Clearly then, this was not exactly an ideal time for any 'holy innocent' to join the human race. It could hardly have been an easy introduction to life, but join, she did and so began the journey of an amazing lady who would go on to survive two major world wars and still retain the spirit to come out at the end with a smile on her face.

If the years during and following those wars were to teach the people of Liverpool anything it was to take life as it comes and enjoy it while you can. There was no room for being too morbid or negative because many things which are out of your control will happen anyway.

Besides all that, such was the devastation and destruction caused by Adolf Hitler's Luftwaffe during their incessant bombing and the May blitz of the city in the Second World War there was so much cleaning and tidying up to do anyway.

Lily was always a resourceful and enterprising kid and in those days there was an old custom where if children visited the house to pay respect to someone who had died, they would always receive some pennies from the grieving family.

And of course due to all that was going on in the world there were plenty of dead bodies to be visited in the area.

So, Lily accompanied by her mate would set out around the district to visit all the dead bodies they could find.

The proceeds of this little enterprise would keep them supplied with sweets for weeks at a time.

That little tale which she liked so much to tell

illustrates the enterprise, spirit and durability which were beginning to form within this special one.

Having said all this she would be quick to point out there was nothing 'remotely romantic' about the conditions people had to endure within those days when Britain was at war. Despite what the broadcasters and journalists of today may portray there was immense hardship and suffering which people of her age had to deal with. Many millions would survive these years bearing the terrible scars and traumas of a time which now becomes so easy and convenient to forget.

Whatever the message Lily was attempting to get across to her listeners, the audience would quickly become enchanted by the honest and straightforward delivery of her talking and would 'bless every breath that she took', in between her speaking so that she would continue to go on and on, keeping them eagerly awaiting the next twist in the tale.

The Halligans had eight children with Lily being one of the eldest. Three of her brothers were lost through drowning, two of them in the war, on the same ship, and one of them; Buster Halligan was only 16 years old. The other lad drowned in the Leeds Liverpool canal.

Still, Lily had the strength to handle all this, she was a remarkable woman.

Lily was a worker, a real worker and that's for sure. She gave over fifty years of her life to working.

The first thirty-nine years were spent in the employment of The British American Tobacco Company, based in the northern docklands area of the city and then the last fourteen years of her working life she spent being employed by the Mersey Docks and Harbour Board, or the MDHB for short, as it was known locally.

In those days there were no 'easy rides' soft jobs were

unheard of and mostly the work was hard, laborious and tiresome. Shift work often took place and the hours were the same for women as well as men

By today's standards life was harsh and sometimes brutal, but Lily always managed to put on a brave face and make light of her own problems allowing her remarkable spirit to rub off on those around her.

Perhaps she was able to realise and understand that there were those out there who were giving up their 'todays' so that we could experience and enjoy our 'tomorrows'.

To get an insight into the resilience that Lily possessed we can learn from one of her many stories which she would delight in telling to her extended family at The Lily Centre.

When her house was bombed during one of the many German air raids the city had to endure, the damage was so bad that the family had to be moved to the outskirts of the city around the Kirkby area in order to keep them safe.

As can be imagined during the war year's public transport was very poor and in some areas did not even exist so Lily found herself in a dilemma: "How am I going to get to work, what am I going to do?"

Lily's workplace was located right in the middle of Adolf Hitler's target area and so of course was in great danger of being bombed as well.

But that did not deter Lily. Amidst the rubble of burnt out and bombed out buildings, alongside the chaos of the blackouts which prevailed throughout the docklands, Lily decided to move back into the old bombed house.

Why on earth was she prepared to do this? "It was the start of the early shifts and I didn't want to be late for work".

This little story often told with a large dose of humility and an even larger dose of humour just about epitomises the wonderful spirit, durability and strength that this very special human being possessed.

Lily's tales and stories about her earlier life and her ability to recall in 'graphic detail' the events in which she became involved would become legendary in the Scotland Road area where her audiences would hang on to every word she said.

Delivered with no small touch of mischievous humour and sometimes reaching the hilarious, Lily had the ability to very quickly lift a gathering of souls out of the doldrums and into a good natured, noisy debate where others were given the impetus and inspiration to recall their own stories, which they would share with the rest of those present.

There was very little room in the wardrobe of her mind for sombre thought.

Lily loved a laugh and a joke, her sense of fun was infectious and her presence within any company, regardless of who they were, was sure to create issues for some and raucous laughter for others.

On one particular occasion the eminent and right honourable Member of Parliament Louise Ellerman was due to visit The Lily Centre. As MP for the area, Louise was prepared to show her support and applaud a brilliant initiative.

On the day of the visit a bouquet of flowers was prepared as a token of welcome to Louise on her visit to The Lily Centre. The idea was to get Lily to present the flowers to Louise as she ended her visit. But Lily thought the flowers were for her!

Eventually, the pair met and enjoyed for some time a very engaging conversation.

At the end of the hour long meeting Lily needed a little prod to remind her to present the bouquet of flowers to Louise. To which she responded, "Who's Louise?"

This reply could only have come from Lily.

On another occasion when Lily was invited alongside other members of The Lily Centre to the opening of the Aintree Breast Cancer Unit, based at Walton Hospital. She was pleased to find out that she would be meeting television star Anne Robinson who had agreed to open the new unit.

Lily carefully prepared for the event. A new coat was purchased together with a beautiful dress and matching bag and shoes. She then spent hours having her hair done and when she was finished looked an absolute picture, with everyone admiring her lovely appearance.

A marvellous time followed at the unit where many people complimented Lily on how well she was looking. Lily even won a new fan, Anne Robinson. Anne seemed so enthralled by Lily's tales and she spent most of her time chatting away to Lily.

When Lily who was by now feeling the heat in the new building, decided to take her coat off one of the girls noticed something.

"Lily," she said, "you've got your dress on back to front".

"Oh yes, I know", she replied.

"I had a ciggie burn in the front so I turned it around so no one would notice".

That was Lily all over, not a care in the world for pomp and ceremony, or even celebrity.

"It was just our Lily." Peggy and Winnie describe the unforgettable night at Liverpool's 'Newz Bar', where Lily upstaged all the stars.

Obviously, The Lily Centre needs assistance and support from the community otherwise it couldn't exist. Paul Flanagan had very kindly put on a high class fashion show to be staged at his glitzy Newz Bar, the cream of Liverpool's nightspots where a galaxy of stars like to frequent on a regular basis.

All the proceeds raised that night would go to The Lily Centre.

Peggy and Winnie decided to treat Lily on this big occasion. They wanted her to feel like the 'Queen Mother', which to them of course she was. A limousine was kindly donated for the evening, one of those with the blacked out windows to take her downtown where she could be dropped off right outside the Newz Bar just like the VIPs'.

Now, just about the same time the rumours were flying all over town that Stella McCartney would be attending the show; the paparazzi were out in force, queuing outside the Newz Bar entrance hoping to catch a shot of Stella and any other VIPs which they could catch.

Lily of course was completely oblivious to the goings on as she climbed into her limousine to begin the short journey to town.

The limousine eventually arrived within a few yards of the red carpet which was rolled out from a packed Newz Bar entrance and when the paparazzi got wind of the arrival the cameras began to flash as if a superstar was about to alight.

There was a rush towards the car as the door, opened by the chauffeur began to reveal the occupant.

Now Lily had been able to see out but the photographers could not see into the car because of the blacked out windows.

Then, with all the elegance of a celebrity star Lily began her entrance before the waiting crowd. As she arose from the cars plush seats the cameras flashed all over the place, as they would for one so famous.

Once on her feet, Lily smiled and waved happily to the media gathering as she danced along the red carpet and into the swish surroundings of the Newz Bar to enjoy a wonderful night of fund raising with the stars.

The news crews outside were left scratching their heads.

At the end of the day it all comes down to contribution, a giving of what you have, to those who need it the most.

There were and are many entertainers and comics, with Liverpool breeding some of the best who have captivated their audiences with tales of fun and laughter.

But there are none who can display a route to a new way of life and understanding like Lily managed to do.

It was her tales and stories about life in the hard times, lovingly refined and described which provided the hope and inspiration for those around her at the time who could take forward her simple message. "Enjoy your life, have fun no matter what tomorrow brings."

Lily was like a mother to Winnie and Peggy she became their mentor, passing on her wisdom and experiences as well as galvanising them in their battles to bring some fun and comfort to the ever growing gatherings of women who were looking for a way forward.

CHAPTER SEVEN

TEAMWORK

Alongside delivering such an important service that The Lily Centre provides. Peggy and Winnie are also involved in very busy family lives, therefore leaving both women with very little time for themselves.

In fact it is the ongoing valuable support from both families that has enabled them to continue to do what they do best.

Winnie Keating often makes the point: "If it wasn't for our husbands, there would be no Lily Centre".

Most people don't want even to imagine the terrifying feeling somebody goes through when they are told that the person most close to them is suffering from a life threatening condition.

Both Tommy Keating and Peter O'Brien had to go through a nightmare of denial, panic, trauma and devastation before they were able to come to terms with the reality of a situation which they now found themselves in.

I know exactly how they felt. And I can only describe this sort of experience as the most stressful period any normal human being has to encounter. Once you are made aware of this dreadful news your life suddenly enters a world of broken hearts and yours is the most broken of all.

So this was the news that both Tommy and Peter had to cope with after picking themselves off the canvas, dragging themselves onto the ropes and dusting themselves down, ready to fight again. And that is what they did.

Tommy recalls: "It was all going on inside, I had a feeling of blind panic. It was the worst feeling in the world when I heard the word cancer. But I couldn't let Winnie see that, I didn't want to upset her more than she already was".

He shows typical Scotland Road spirit when he remembers: "It never crossed my mind that Winnie wasn't going to make it".

Tommy goes on to pay tribute to the children; James, Paul, Julie and Clare, for their valuable support but adds: "I believe a man's role is to support, let them know they can depend on you. You can shut your mind to it or accept it and make things as easy as you can".

He continues: "We were close before, but we are stronger for it and I am so proud of her for what she has gone through. It amazes me how Winnie just got on with it, without complaining. I am just glad that I could be there for her".

Tommy Keating's remarks portray a perfect illustration of how the close knit family can play such an important role in the recovery of a seriously ill patient.

Having endured the initial emotional upheaval and the physical pain that Winnie would have to suffer, the family went on to display amazing strength and courage while providing the necessary back up and support which she needed in order to continue with her fight.

Not very far from the stricken Keating household there was a very similar, distressing situation at the home of the O'Brien family developing.

Peggy O'Brien had received the same awful news that Winnie Keating had received and her loved ones had struggled to cope with those early darkest hours every bit as much as the Keating's did.

Peter O'Brien recalls: "This was the toughest experience of my life. There is nothing else you can do but support them, practically and emotionally. But at first I found it difficult to accept. I suppose I was in denial at the time. I was just shocked and wouldn't accept it, I didn't want to believe it was true".

Peter was clearly trying to cope with severe trauma and the worst possible blow that can hit the male head of a family.

"How am I going to tell Peter, John and Steven?" His three sons, was one of the first questions he asked of himself.

"At first I couldn't say anything; will she get through it? All sorts of things go through your mind. But then, I thought, well Peggy is a fighter, if anyone can get through it she will, she's strong willed. I just remember telling myself, I just had to be there for her. You feel helpless, but you're not. I was frightened for her but I couldn't let her see that".

There were times when his brave front would come down. "But that was only when I was on my own. I never let Peggy see it because I didn't want to upset her".

Peter's comments here help to put into perspective the magnitude of effect which such devastating news has upon ordinary families and not least in the way that they pick themselves up from the floor, ready to carry on battling regardless of the odds stacked against them. A truly outstanding spirit.

Strangers when we meet

So, here we have an outline story of two families, and how they were brought together.
- Both born and bred and living within close proximity to each other.
- Both stricken by the female head of the family suffering from the same life threatening condition.

- Both women coming together having not crossed each others path for over fifty years.
- Both families showing a resolve and determination to do battle, not just for themselves, but eventually for many thousands of others against this debilitating disease.
- Both families providing a teamwork approach, leaving their own priorities on hold for another day, while these two remarkable women went to work in building up what is now the most successful breast cancer aftercare initiative in the country.

A story then of courage, bravery and humanity, all rolled into a helter-skelter of life, lived on a day to day basis, by the durable people of Liverpool's Scotland Road.

A story made even more remarkable when you consider that these two families who, although being born and bred within the same area were strangers to each other until they were suddenly brought together by fate.

Especially so, when it is taken into account that both Peggy and Winnie fathers were in fact classmates at Saint Silvester's School off Scotland Road, some seventy years earlier.

I have already expressed my views upon 'The chosen Few', and would make no apology for them, hoping to provoke discussion on the subject of why some people seem more able to cope than others.

Why, in this case? I don't know, but clearly this story shows overwhelming evidence that these two particular families have been able to take the knocks on the chin, then get back up off the floor and start fighting again.

Winnie Keating's Family Tree

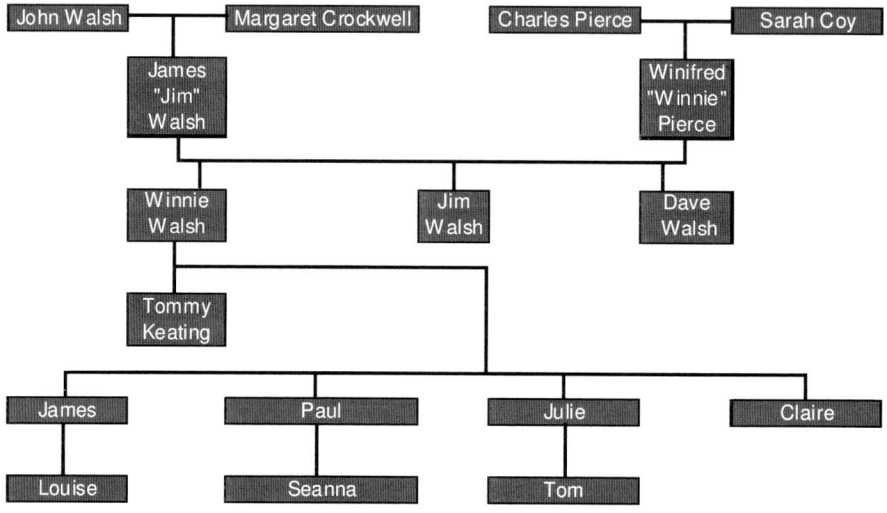

Peggy O'Brien's Family Tree

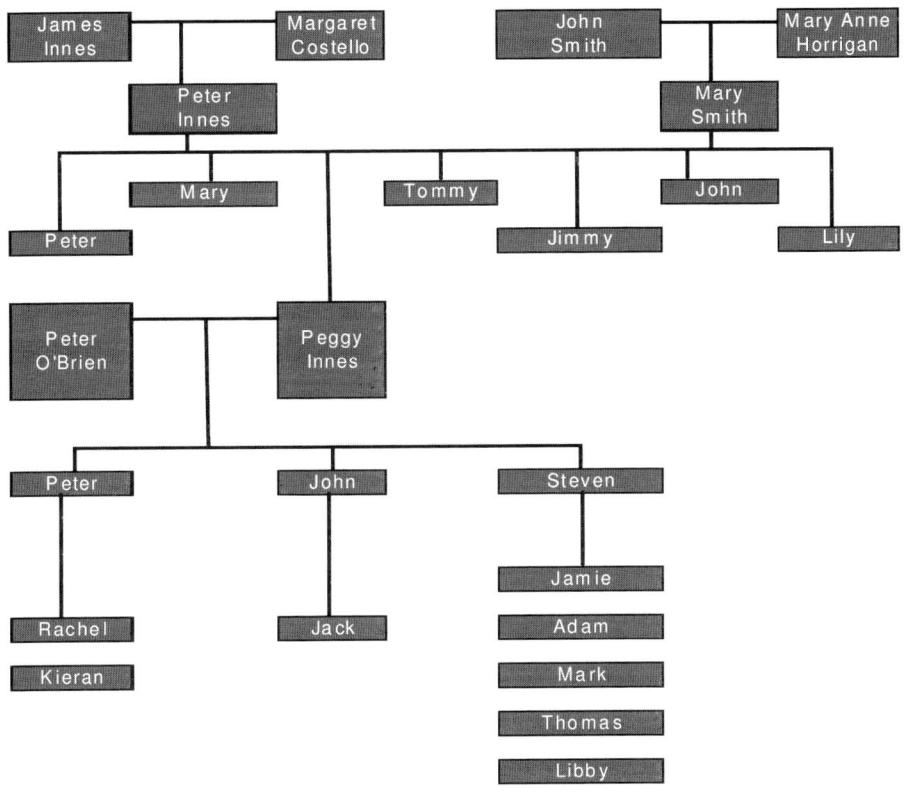

Lily Centre

There's Always Room in Our House

It sits low in the valley overlooking the river and its doors
are wide open for you can come and go.
The welcome is warm and its workers deliver a service
which helps when people are low.
The garden is lovely, a place for the people carefully
watched over by Saint Anthony's Steeple.
So next time you're looking for some goodness to see.
Why not pop in they will make you some tea.
You can always laugh, you can joke, have a butty as well.
You may even have your own story to tell.
And if you start wondering just who was its mentor.
They'll tell you the tale of The Lily Centre.

CHAPTER EIGHT

LILY CENTRE

Nestling just off the west side of Scotland Road at the foothills of Everton valley, deep in the heart of Liverpool's inner city; lies The Lily Centre. Located in a tenement block, three former flats have been carefully converted and refurbished to provide much needed assistance and support as well as social activities and inclusion for people suffering from breast cancer.

This fantastic facility also embraces family and friends in its agenda adding extra benefits such as open discussion on how different people are coping with their various situations and the opportunity for people to mix together and discuss day to day events in a flexible and informal atmosphere.

Other benefits like trips to the seaside, holidays, days out and function nights all carried out in a well organised manner also give people the feeling of belonging to an extended family where they can talk openly about their worries, fears, hopes and aspirations.

Self expression is positively encouraged alongside a culture of promoting participation in the general running of the facility. This helps to breed confidence and feelings of self worth amongst all those involved.

The emotional and physical rewards have been outstanding and will continue to be so because of a renewed sense of purpose instilled within those who benefit and contribute towards the initiative. People who are involved don't have the time to be lonely anymore.

The Lily Centre crosses the class, political, religious and racial divides in that it does not matter who you are or where you come from, there's a welcome on the mat.

The upbeat atmosphere around the place generated by the smiling, happy faces who meet within its walls actually create a contradiction to the reality of the situation which most of them find themselves in.

These convivial surroundings enable people to share and deal with their own and each others problems in a positive and practical manner.

The Lily Garden

Sometimes it seems that rain keeps falling.
Like heavens tears.
Then suddenly the sun begins to shine.
And the grass begins to grow again.
A state of happiness commences as the flowers in our garden show their bloom.

The Lily Centre's Garden of Remembrance is now a firmly established place of beauty.

At its height the garden displays a wonderful array of colour with its many flowers and plants blooming for all to enjoy as they bask in the sunshine and sway with the summer breeze.

Looking out onto Scotland Road facing the church of Saint Anthony, The Lily Centre garden provides a source of pleasure to church goers, passers by and of course those who attend the centre.

It is also a peaceful haven, flourishing in the midst of a sprawling inner city area, where people can spend some time to cherish the memory of the ones that they hold dear, who have now moved on to a better place.

I love that garden, it is so beautiful. It has done wonders for the local community as well as providing an aura of tranquillity for those who find so much comfort in finding themselves amongst the flowers.

The garden becomes even more significant when one becomes aware of the tremendous amount of effort which was put in to create it.

A trip along the coast to the Southport Flower Show gave the group an opportunity to scavenge many of the flowers and plants from the stalls at the show that now adorn Lily's garden.

The group packed as many donated plants as they could handle on to the bus back home so they could build their place of peace from scratch.

They were on their hands and knees working like beavers until nightfall so that the garden could be opened on time. By the time they were finished everyone was covered in soil from head to toe.

Opening day threatened to be a washout as dark clouds loomed during the morning, which created some apprehension. But they need not have worried. When it came to the time to open the garden the sun shone with brilliance.

CHAPTER NINE

A SIGHT FOR SORE EYES

I will always remember that beautiful summer's day, some eight years ago when I first had the privilege of setting eyes upon The Lily Centre. We were busy working within a massive government project aimed at providing decent social housing for the mainly frail and elderly tenants who had suffered some dreadful living conditions, having to exist in some of the worst sub standard housing in Western Europe

The morning had been manic and my team were run off their feet as the phones continued to ring. Major works were now taking place in order to provide warm, dry, safe and secure accommodation for thousands of people whose homes had become uninhabitable due to lack of effective maintenance. Part of our job was to ensure that they made the necessary moves to new or temporary homes with the minimum of trauma and hassle which usually occurs while this situation exists.

My phone rang, yet again, as Maria informed me: "It's Julian Flanagan for you".

"Okay, thanks Maria", I replied.

Julian was the youngest member of the Flanagan family who were working with us, as contractors, to help us achieve a successful conclusion to the project.

"Hello Frank, how are you doing?" Julian's ever pleasant disposition greeted me.

"Up the damn wall, Julian; up the damn wall", I answered.

He laughed at my response, knowing that I used to swear too much in those days, partly due to a failure to express myself properly and partly due to self inflicted pressure which I would place myself under. However, he never used to take too much notice.

"I just wondered," he continued, "Do you have an hour at lunch time? There is something that we have become involved with that I'd like you too see".

"Er, well, why not", I replied, thinking, well it would do me good to get out of the office for an hour or so.

And so it followed that Julian picked me up from the housing office, based in Great homer Street, around midday to take me on the short journey along Scotland Road to Woodstock Street, where he wanted to show me the new development that Paul, his elder brother had embarked upon.

It consisted of a three storey block of flats which had been left to run down but were now being refurbished to a high 'decent homes' specification.

As the car came to a halt in the car park of the tenements, we both wiped the sweat from our brows opening both doors to enjoy the cooling sea breeze that was gently blowing eastwards from the river Mersey.

The warm summer sun beats down on us as Julian explained: "This is the very place which I thought you would like to see, it's The Lily Centre".

I remembered the name because of previous conversations with Paul who was aware that I was a child of Scotland Road, and so knew of my interest in such a project. Little, at that point, did I realise though, just how much progress had been made.

The Lily Centre was located on the ground floor of this block of flats and extensive refurbishment had already been carried out to the premises.

As Julian and I entered through the front door, he remarked: "They just needed somewhere to meet, so Paul gave them this flat".

My eyes were scanning the scene in front of me; I was in a word flabbergasted.

The whole area was beautiful. Lot's of elderly people, young and old, men and women were milling around, laughing, joking, having tea, coffee, butties and biscuits; chatting away to one another, they hardly noticed Julian and I had entered the building.

"All of these people are suffering from breast cancer", Julian informed me. "So, when Peggy came to see Paul to see if we could help he just said, yeah, okay have this if you want it. So now they've got it".

I was by this time, gobsmacked. It had become clear to me from this very early stage that something awesome was beginning to happen. Here were a group of people whose lives had been handed a terrible blow, yet here they were chatting happily, cheerfully and enthusiastically together over tea, coffee and biscuits; within a place in which they were entirely comfortable.

This was just because a few other people had recognised their problem, decided that they were in a position to help, then just went for it. Simple as that!

At that moment, on that day, I knew that I had been 'Lillied!'

My first introduction to The Lily Centre would have a deep and lasting effect upon how I looked at life in the future, for it provided me with a smart kick up the backside, educated me very quickly, and taught me to recognise complacency in the future. It reminded me of my 'Ninnies' living room where all the girls from the neighbourhood, young and old alike, would gather to enjoy a laugh and a cup of tea together, while being busy gossiping about everyone and everything.

Peggy and Winnie hardly noticed us; they were preoccupied with everyone else and were busy mingling amongst the company ensuring everyone was comfortable. I would imagine that they thought that I was just another 'suit' who Julian had invited down to have a look at what was going on. That could not have been further from the truth, I was totally taken in by what I had seen.

Yes, I had been Lillied! So much so that I have been involved in some capacity ever since and have been full of admiration for the likes of Paul, Julian, John and Kathleen Flanagan for their continuous effort in sustaining Peggy and Winnie for so long, which has played a massive part in bringing the initiative to where it is today.

There is something unique here, something different, yet so simple. It took me back to those post war years where people looked after each other, where everyone 'mucked in' to play their part for the benefit of all concerned.

It reminded me of the steadfast will to survive displayed by our parents and grandparents during the cities darkest days, and how much we could learn from their courage and bravery if we put our minds to it.

No yards and yards of paperwork.

No meaningless policy and procedures.

No bureaucratic bungling.

It was simply a basic human instinct to survive whilst keeping an extended family together almost daring the world to part them. What was my privilege to see on that beautiful summer's day some eight years ago was indeed A sight for sore eyes!

They say I'm not well

They think I may cry

They give me some medicines

To help me get by

But they don't really know me

They can't read my mind

For I'll go on fighting to stay part of mankind

So don't write me off just yet

It's too early, too soon

Because let me remind you

It's not all doom and gloom.

CHAPTER TEN

LET THE PEOPLE HAVE THEIR SAY

"It's not all doom and gloom having cancer; it doesn't mean you can't have a laugh."

Peggy

"Very low at diagnosis time, I admit."

Peggy

"When you are diagnosed you think you are on your own and the night time is always the worst. Your family can be marvellous and very supportive but there's no substitute for talking to someone else who knows exactly what you're going through."

Peggy

"I went down and just peeked my head in the door; there were just five of us. Within a few weeks that number had doubled to ten."

Winnie

"Peggy was already in the room when I arrived. We could immediately see that a support group like that was needed. We knew even then that we needed more than two hours on a Monday. We weren't really a formal group we had no chair person or anything, but we were just friends, sitting around and having a chat."

Winnie

"I remember calling in to see Mike McDonald the local housing officer based at the Cramner Street housing office, to ask if he could help to provide, maybe a hard to let property which we could adapt. He couldn't do anything but he did say he knew someone who may be able to help and he introduced Winnie and me to Paul Flanagan."

Peggy

"I tell this story all the time and still can't believe it's true. He shook hands, said come with me in my car and brought me along here. He opened the door and said "Look, this is for you if you want it."

Peggy

"When we moved in we had nothing, not even a teaspoon."

Peggy

"We knew from our own experiences what the families go through and I think they even go through more than us. Although we help over seven hundred women, you can treble that because of the relatives and carers who come to the centre."

Peggy

"We have become established in the area and people know who we are."

Peggy

"I'd say that the city of Liverpool and its female inhabitants need more Lily Centres somewhere none threatening, none medical and frankly a bit of fun."

Susan Lee, Liverpool Echo

"There are those who turn their face away from life's challenges, preferring to hide under a table with eyes tight shut, hoping that whatever the nasty thing is, it will go away. Others roll up their sleeves, square up their shoulders and prepare to do battle."

Susan Lee, Liverpool Echo

"Alan would ring me from all parts of the country as he used to spend a lot of time travelling around doing after dinner speeches. He would be really enthusiastic and say "I've just been telling so and so about the wonderful initiative that The Lily Centre is and they would like to know more about it up here in Scotland, for instance."

Winnie: on Alan Ball

"We could never have achieved what we have managed to do so without the support of our husbands, not many men would put up with the time we spend out of the house, Without Tommy or Peter there would be no Lily Centre."

Winnie

"Peter has always encouraged me to carry on, having to attend this or that function or meeting on a cold dark night when it would be easier to stay in the warm, sometimes its not easy."

Peggy

"I can't get over the fact that our name: "The Lily Centre", also stands for tender loving care for example TLC which as we all know is universal and is exactly what The Lily Centre is all about."

Eileen Rogan

"Alan would pop in at morning time to see how we were doing. He had it timed to perfection, that when he arrived we would be preparing tea and toast. He loved our toast and would wolf it down as he chatted away."

Winnie: on Alan Ball

"After hearing about The Lily Centre at one of Everton's functions we found out that Everton Football Club could find a few things to help along The Lily Centre to auction and we have enjoyed it ever since."

Dave Hickson

"They were magical; there was something in the spirit of those two women that was amazing. You can't fail to want to help."

Pauline Daniels

"The Lily Centre provides a lifeline for anyone who is diagnosed with breast cancer. Founders Winnie Keating and Peggy O'Brien are amazing human beings who planted a small seed a decade ago and have built the charity into a Liverpool institution which has reached out and helped people around the world. In many ways The Lily Centre typifies the people of Liverpool – it is generous, selfless and has a heart of gold. I will do all I can to help."

Warren Bradley, Leader of Liverpool City Council

"Cancer haunts and stalks, it is with you twenty four hours a day, seven days a week and affects every aspect of life.

When my two beautiful ladies, my wife and my daughter were diagnosed within six weeks of each other, I was helpless.

All I could do was to try and support, as when this disease strikes, it has no feelings for anybody. It was their inner strength that constantly amazed me. Believe me; Lesley was braver than any footballer I have ever played against.

I come from a long line of men who went out to work, brought home the money that provided food for the table and put their feet up before going to the pub to meet their mates. I am no 'New Age Man', my role was to provide a house, food and clothes. That was the way I lived my life, and Lesley, being a northern girl, was used to that and demanded nothing more.

She laughed at me when I had to adapt.

I had to change light bulbs and put washing in the machine. I had to learn what the knobs represented.

Financial matters used to baffle me, although I can work out a 'Yankee' racing-bet in seconds.

Lesley was with me though. I needed her there as I needed her all my life.

She was my friend, lover, wife and guardian angel. Who knows where my life would have wandered, had it not been for her mental strength and loyal devotion, as the mother of three, great children she took the credit for making them what they are.

No matter what I had ever achieved on the football field. No matter what I had done for England. No matter whether I had money or a big house it didn't matter.

So, as you can imagine. I was very, very happy to be associated with the hard work that you do at The Lily

Centre, giving up your own free time.

It's a marvellous, marvellous idea and it's marvellous of everyone connected to The Lily Centre to be involved. I just wanted to be a little part of it."

Alan Ball
1945–2007

The People's Charity. Created by the people. Financed by the people. For the people

Ryley Forrester

"My aunt died of breast cancer and she was a local woman so there are particular connections here for me.

I first met the girls several years ago when they were nominated for Merseyside Women of the Year for their achievements. They really stood out and made a huge impact on me and everyone else, and they still make a great impact on people.

There is something about the atmosphere which brings out the best in people. The idea is a simple one but a special one. I think that it is typical of Peggy and Winnie that they don't want to keep the idea to themselves; they want it to be well known and spread around. The women of London, the North East, Wales and Scotland could replicate it.

In many countries of the world women are still isolated by cultural taboos and do not talk about breasts.

I think this idea really could be spread across the world."

Cherie Booth

"On my numerous visits to the centre I have always been warmly welcomed and have always been struck by the good humour and feeling of well being that pervades the place.

No one would question the extremely valuable work and support offered by The Lily Centre to all who come through their doors; but without doubt if it was not for the dedication, tenacity and endeavours of Peggy and Winnie it quite simply would not be there or indeed continue to exist.

Long may it, and Peggy and Winnie, all continue to enhance and bring hope to the lives of the people who use the centre ...

Peggy and Winnie have got guts; they're fine and feisty, homely just like your mum. They throw a comfort zone around everyone. They are there for support and let's face it; they've been through similar experiences themselves."

Dean Sullivan

"I was first introduced to Peggy and Winnie at The Lily Centre nearly 10 years ago when as captain of Everton Football Club I went to the centre to have a picture taken to help them with their publicity. At that first meeting with the girls I realised they were full of energy and enthusiasm for their cause and on meeting some of the people using the centre saw that they were providing vital care and support for cancer sufferers and the families in the Liverpool area.

Although it deals with sad and traumatic situations, The Lily Centre is predominantly a happy place filled with laughter.

Since then I have been happy to be associated with The Lily Centre and attend as many functions as I can. These occasions are always great nights which Peggy and

Winnie work extremely hard at to make a success and they are enjoyed by a great variety of people from celebrities to those coping with cancer.

I have tried to help with fundraising and in 2005 got sponsorship from friends and family to run the Chicago marathon – which I am still getting over! It was very well supported and well worth the effort when I presented the girls with the cheque at their Christmas party.

The Lily Centre has become a well known and vital support to the cancer patients it serves and it is testimony to Peggy and Winnie and all their supporters that they have managed to keep raising the funds needed to ensure its survival and to make it the success it is."

Dave Watson

"These ordinary women have done an incredible job. You look out of the window into that garden and it's like the Garden of Eden. It's a fabulous place known the length and breadth of Liverpool. It should be known the length and breadth of England.

We need to keep it going, expand it by raising money which is mainly done through donations. That's the hardest part for these two girls."

Ricky Tomlinson

"There are no appointments needed. You can come and go as you please. We like it to be a home from home. You get your support from each other; someone else who has been there. We talk amongst ourselves and we sort of counsel each other."

Peggy

"When you're a twelve year old, working class, Liverpool kid and your Mum is taken from you by breast cancer, it's something that affects you for the rest of your life. In that life I was brought up in Liverpool, joined a comedy group called Scaffold and had a big number 1 hit with a sing-a-long song called 'Lily the Pink'.

So when I first heard of a Breast Cancer Support Centre called The Lily Centre, I naturally had an interest in it, particularly when I discovered it was a Liverpool people's charity, founded by Liverpool people.

Over the years it's been a privilege to get to know the two founders, Peggy (O'Brien) and Winnie (Keating) plus their many dedicated helpers. Unfortunately I never got to meet Lily (Halligan) the lady the centre was named after, who was born in the First World War and died in 2003, but I have an affinity with her because of my mother.

In those old, dark days (of ignorance and fear) Mum and Lily's illnesses were referred to, in whispers, as 'the big C' … if you had it that was that.

If only my Mum had had a place like The Lily Centre to go to in 1956, where she could have discussed her condition openly, to face the reality of her situation with KNOWLEDGE of what was going on … but she didn't. Unaware of what to do in those days, Lily treated herself in secret for seven years, and mum, who was a nurse and midwife … took Bisodol! Possibly hoping it would eventually all go away.

The Lily Centre was created to raise awareness of this destructive disease, to try to demystify it in some small way, and give emotional support for people going through such trauma (which is sadly lacking on the NHS) Lily was its oldest member and she went on to enjoy many more years of life, due to the care and support of the group.

Originally created as a self-help group for women with

breast cancer, it now helps men as, sorry lads, MEN as well as women, suffer from breast cancer i.e. The Lily Centre supports ALL Breast Cancer Sufferers, as well as their family and friends.

I know first hand the importance of support for families who have to cope with such trauma, and then trying to pick up the pieces after your very personal loss.

The Lily Centre is a charity founded and financed by the people … Liverpool people helping sick Liverpool people. It's now, unbelievably TEN years since the girls started their 'Twenty FIVE Hour Service (thank you Flanagan's!) helping people cope with this dreadful disease … some years hanging on by the skin of their teeth!

It would be great to report that after all the work they've done that Winnie and Peggy now have all the money in the world to continue their invaluable work, but the REALITY is that there are no big buck government handouts for The Lily Centre, and these wonderful ladies plus their devoted helpers STILL need help … particularly in our recession!

Even though the centre is now receiving global recognition in Europe, India and America, I like to think 'charity begins at home' and as The Lily Centre is still looking for volunteers and fund raisers … can YOU help in any way?

Thank YOU very much (no pun intended!)".

Mike McCartney

"Once you walk through the doors of The Lily Centre there is no turning back. That lovely friendly feeling of warmth which Peggy and Winnie create is fantastic. They are well and truly selfless in their work and always seem to find time for everybody.

I adore these two girls and will always try to do my best to help as I have done in the past.

Just think of what they could achieve with a bit more support from all of us."

Pauline Daniels

"Not long after they first started out the girls rang me up at Radio Merseyside's A Team, to see if we could help with some equipment as they had very little in those days.

I thought to myself what a lovely idea that they have come up with in helping others like themselves so I decided to go along and see them.

Well I was amazed by what I saw. There was a beautiful feeling about the place, being so warm, inviting and friendly. It was infectious. You could say, there and then that I had been well and truly Lillied!

Peggy and Winnie deserve to be successful in all that they do. In fact these two women should be nominated in the New Year's Honours List."

Estelle Condliff, Radio Merseyside

"I was first introduced to Peggy and Winnie by Dave Lockwood at one of the do's and I was impressed immediately by their sense of humour and open personalities. These two women are fantastic, the work they do is colossal and they happily do it all for nothing.

What also drew me towards them was that my own mother's name was Lily and coming from the area meant that I couldn't help getting involved.

You feel that you have to do something to help.

On visiting The Lily Centre, you would never believe the suffering that these women have been through once you sample the atmosphere. A wonderful place."

Peter McIntosh

"I love coming to see Peggy and Winnie at The Lily Centre. Their infectious enthusiasm rubs off. They are so dedicated in all that they do.

Coming from a medical background myself, gives me a good perception of the major contribution that they are making within this field. Peggy and Winnie are a wonderful inspiration to us all."

Dame Lorna Muirhead, Lord Lieutenant of Liverpool

"When Mike McDonald from the local housing office first mentioned Peggy and Winnie to me, regarding what they were trying to do I made arrangements to meet Peggy with a view to help in any way that we could.

Flanagan's were busy working on a refurbishment project for a block of flats in the Scotland Road area of the city so it seemed sensible to take her there.

It was impossible not to be impressed by her as well as what Winnie and herself were attempting to achieve. I was also reminded of my own mum and the hard work she had put in while bringing our family up.

Peggy and Winnie are so typical of ordinary Liverpool mums everywhere. They have a tremendous passion for what they do both being genuine and so honest. They are not in your face, as their actions speak louder than any words.

I remember at the time how humble I felt when I realised the passion that they displayed in attempting to do some good.

Anyway, having showed Peggy a ground floor flat in the complex I said, 'Look this is for you, for as long as you want it'.

It was the least we could do. So in a very subtle way I had been 'Lillied' at a very early stage.

Now that they have come this far more help is needed to allow them to spread this fantastic message throughout this country and overseas."

Paul Flanagan

"Montse and I give our fullest support to The Lily Centre, and pay tribute to the committed and dedicated work of Winnie, Peggy and their volunteers these past ten years.

The centre means a lot to both of us, but more so to hundreds of people that have been offered the warm and welcoming hand of understanding to help them through their most difficult times.

Congratulations on the launch of this book, *You've been Lillied!* Which has been written to commemorate these last ten years – What a great title?

Winnie, Peggy and The Lily Centre will always be close to our hearts."

Rafa and Montse Benitez

CHAPTER ELEVEN

COINCIDENCES. OR IS IT MEANT TO BE?

Sometimes things happen which can seem strange and extraordinary to some people while others may pass off these happenings as mere coincidence.

Both Peggy and Winnie's fathers, Jimmy Walsh and Peter Innes were born in 1921 within twenty-four hours of each other and were in the same class together at school.

Peggy and Winnie were born in 1949 within a week of each other.

Peggy and Winnie's grandchildren Jack and Louise were born within a week of each other.

Louise's birthday is on the anniversary of Lily's funeral.

Peggy and Winnie received the keys to The Lily Centre from Paul Flanagan right in the middle of their birthday week on 7 June 2000. It was the week they were celebrating their respective birthdays.

Even though living just a few streets away from each other and being the same age, Peggy and Winnie had never met until they came together to found The Lily Centre.

Their paths must have crossed a thousand times while living and working locally most of their lives.

Another amazing coincidence which crosses the international divide lies in the words of Lily Halligan spoken in October 2001 and the words of Montse Benitez, within her statement six years later when applauding the work of The Lily Centre.

Lily: "If a woman discovered she had a lump in her breast, she very often keeps it to herself. She might not even talk to her family, partly through fear and partly because nobody spoke about it. It wasn't the sort of thing that people talked about. If people did talk about it, it would be in hushed tones. People couldn't even say the word cancer; it was referred to as 'the big C'. A lot of people didn't really know an awful lot about it. Thank goodness things are different today and people are more aware, it means women can get help earlier."

What should be remembered here is that Montse Benitez had not long moved to England from Spain and was still in the process of understanding and speaking English which makes her words all the more remarkable when the similarities to Lily's words are considered.

Montse: "I have had friends and relatives who have suffered from breast cancer, but for most people in Spain, cancer is seen as a private illness so you tend not to have centres and meetings or those kinds of things. We have official hospital care but afterwards it becomes more difficult because cancer is something that no one wants to talk about. It is important to have a place like this where people can talk openly about their illness and help each other".

When looked at in this context, two different women from different countries who didn't speak the same language, producing words and opinions some six years apart which were so close in delivering the same message. Even though they could not have known each other this all makes for another amazing and remarkable 'coincidence'.

CHAPTER TWELVE

SPECIAL SPANISH ANGELS
THE HOLY TRINITY

When Fernando Torres took off his original Liverpool shirt the first thing he did was to autograph it and write a special message, 'To The Lily Centre, my first Liverpool shirt – Fernando Torres'.

Peggy O'Brien later commented, "What a wonderful gesture".

Rafa Benitez later took the shirt along to Paul Flanagan's 'Newz Bar' so that a raffle could be held to raise some much needed funds for the centre. Paul said at the time, "We provided the charity with its original premises but they have outgrown that now and we are trying to raise funds to help them buy their own property".

Montse Benitez became a patron of The Lily Centre despite some early hilarious language barriers. Grappling at the time with the broad Scouse accents Montse misunderstood what she was being asked. "I thought they were asking me to become a patient", laughed Montse when Peggy and Winnie attempted to describe to her the role of a patron. Once it dawned upon all three women raucous laughter filled the air and Montse has since done a great job.

"You should have seen the look on her face", laughed Peggy. "She looked really confused and we couldn't work out what was wrong, until she said she didn't want to be a patient. We all just fell about laughing, and then we explained that we wanted her to be a patron, not a patient and she accepted straight away".

Montse had been invited by Paul Flanagan to get involved with The Lily Centre and she did so straight away. "I like helping people and it is good to be given the opportunity to be able to help an organisation which is so special", Montse continued, "Rafa is the same, but he has much less time. I had heard of The Lily Centre because it does so much good work in Liverpool but I had never met the girls. So when Paul asked me if I wanted to get involved I said yes, straight away".

Winnie recalls, "From the moment we met Montse we knew she was perfect for us. She's a really nice person and gets on well with people, and she wants to help. What more could we ask for? She has been fantastic for us and with her contributions we hope we can make a real difference to even more people".

Montse who is just so happy to help concludes, "It's good to be involved in something like this because it is important to so many people. The Lily Centre does wonderful work so if I can help in some small way I will be delighted".

And so it goes to show that there is overwhelming evidence provided by people from all walks of life, from every persuasion and background, who once they 'get Lillied', are prepared to give time and effort and support to such a simple but unique initiative which has now become so firmly entrenched within the history of this city.

CHAPTER THIRTEEN

MIND OVER MATTER

One of the major factors which often seems to be ignored within the NHS provision, and indeed throughout successive governments is that the state of a patients emotional health plays a massive part in their recovery or otherwise.

When someone is informed that they may be suffering from a life threatening illness, it is reasonable to expect them to go through a degree of trauma which will have an effect on both themselves and their families.

But where are the policies, procedures and budget provision which would help to address these issues? They don't seem to exist.

How is it then that Peggy and Winnie, two ordinary housewives from Scotland Road have recognised and championed the need for such a service, over all these years while the suits at the top level don't even seem to recognise emotional issues? The mind boggles!

The care of a patient's emotional wellbeing is the most fundamental part of the service which Peggy and Winnie provide and so is the prime reason for their success so far.

There is overwhelming evidence here to support the belief that people react in a positive way when given emotional support while attempting to confront and come to terms with their physical condition. If only the suits in authority could realise that they would save untold millions of tax payers money as well as improving the quality of life in patients if they were to channel some thought into people's emotional wellbeing and the part that it plays in overall recovery.

They can learn a lot from Peggy and Winnie. We can only speculate why such a basic common sense approach is widely ignored, perhaps the service users are not great on politics. Perhaps they are not regarded as important enough. Perhaps the issue is not a vote catcher.

Whatever the reason, Peggy and Winnie have proved time and time again that attention and support given to a person's emotional state when they are low or in trauma goes a long way in assisting their future chances of becoming well again.

Lily Halligan herself was given a massive boost from the emotional support which she received from Peggy and Winnie, after being so afraid and frightened to talk about her condition, her own confidence gradually grew enough for her to be able to enjoy the rest of her life having a good laugh along the way.

She was also able to transmit that earlier health and support on to others around her and to pass on the message and benefits which she had received to great effect.

"Once we are able to get people talking about themselves, we then know that they will soon be sharing a joke with us".
Winnie.

"When we get a new woman in everything stops for her because we know how hard it is. You think you are on your own so we try to build up her confidence straight away".
Peggy.

What Peggy and Winnie are proving all the time is that with the right approach, support and attention, people are responding positively in their attitude to and their education about breast cancer by being part of The Lily Centre.

Once people begin to get better, they become more able to do things for themselves and so become less of a liability to the states finances. Finances which many of us have paid into during most of our working lives could then be used in a more practical way such as funding some of the emotional health issues already mentioned.

When The Going Gets Tough

Big and black those clouds may be

But I will blow them away from me

And I will blow them so far away
they will never trouble you

So far away I will blow that your skies will be clear
and you will see the sun

And your sun will be the same sun
that I was lucky enough to see when I was like you

"Blessed are the weak and the sick
for one day they will be in paradise"

Do not be afraid for I am with you.

CHAPTER FOURTEEN

WHEN THE GOING GETS TOUGH, THE TOUGH GET GOING

Why is it that so many healthy people find it hard to even comprehend the thought of becoming ill? And why is it that those of us who do become ill and some of us seriously ill display a bravery and acceptance of their own situation which can put the rest of us to shame.

The story of those who show tremendous character and strength in the face of adversity continues to defy common logic. The facts are straight forward, people suffering illness and disability have in some cases been able to show an inner strength and capacity for survival which will forever captivate and inspire the rest of their healthy counterparts toward living a more stable and responsible life.

I cried because I had no shoes until I met someone with no feet. Are then these brave and inspirational souls the ultimate sacrifice the human race has to offer in order for the rest of us to become better people?

If that is the case, maybe we all need to look in the mirror and come face to face with a reality check when deciding what is important to us and what contributions we are making towards the benefit and well being of our communities as a whole.

Some people regard illness as a weakness and that can only be a shame but there are too many who feel this way. Perhaps the majority of us who have these negative feelings are just scared of being sick ourselves and so become dismissive of the subject brushing it under the carpet so it will go away. But it won't!

Just a few short steps towards recognising that sick people actually exist can be the beginning of a more positive and healthy view of the world in which we live.

As Peggy O'Brien has stated on many occasions, "It doesn't have to be doom and gloom".

Clearly she has displayed the benefits of remaining positive over many years of adversity.

Being scared or afraid is not a sin. Lily Halligan was so frightened of her illness that she wouldn't go to the doctors for treatment, in fear of having to face up to the inevitable bad news. It was only later in her life that Lily came to terms with her condition and was able to go on to help create a fantastic atmosphere of hope and aspirations with her extended family at The Lily Centre.

Winnie Keating has explained her misgivings and doubts of the early days about whether or not a self-help group would work. She was afraid at the time of not being of any use to such a group and so nearly never joined. Something changed her mind however, and that something then changed the course of Liverpool's history. For this we should all be truly thankful.

Peggy O'Brien tells of how she feared the night time and the feeling of being very low during the time after being diagnosed with the illness. She gradually gained the strength and confidence to pick herself up, dust herself down and come out fighting on all fronts, as she still does today to keep the community together.

So it follows that being scared or frightened is a natural human feeling which affects us all at some time or other in different ways depending on the circumstances in which we find ourselves.

Lily's early sense of fear was real and genuine, but it

The Lily Centre Photo Album

Peggy, Winnie and Pat at Liverpool Town Hall, 2004.

Afternoon tea with Lady Mayoress, Moira Roderick.

Pauline Fleming, Roger Phillips and Eithne Brown attend a charity event at St George's Hall, September 2004.

Jimmy and Ann with Ricky and Rita Tomlinson at St George's Hall, September 2004.

Dave Lockwood, the Hollyoaks girls and Jason McAteer at St George's Hall, September 2004.

Kathleen Flanagan and Maria Hill at the Park Hotel.

Estelle Condliff, Sue Lee, Winnie, Cherie Booth, Peggy, Pauline Daniels and Pat Heron at the Park Hotel.

Mike and Joan McDonald.

Pauline Daniels and Eithne Brown.

Paul Duvall, Brian Dodds and Jen Heyes.

Peter and Colette McIntosh with Peter and Shiela Quigley.

Tim Gretsby of VLM Airlines with Cherie Booth and Warren Bradley.

Pat, Peggy, Lady Mayoress Joan Lang and Winnie.

Peggy, Lady Mayoress Joan Lang, Cherie and Winnie.

Julian Flanagan, Cherie, Paul and Grace Flanagan at the Park Hotel.

Dave and Pat Hickson.

All the patrons at the Park Hotel, 2007.

Peter and Peggy O'Brien with Winnie and Tommy Keating.

Dave Hickson and Cherie Booth with Mitzy Muller and her daughter Letitia and Pat Hickson at the Park Hotel.

Peggy, Estelle Condliff and Winnie.

Winnie and Peggy ...

... at the Annual Garden Party, 2008.

Winnie and Peggy with Pat Heron.

Peggy, Dave and Winnie in the Lily Garden, 2004.

Dave and Pat Hickson in the Lily Garden, August 2004.

Pamela Tibb and Mike McCartney at the garden party.

John Gorman and Mike McCartney, showing their support for the Lily Centre, 2007.

Breast Cancer Awareness Month, October 2006.

Christmas card from Cherie and Tony.

XXX

Montse Benitez with Peggie, Winnie and Warren Bradley at the *Local Heroes Award*, December 2008.

Winnie, Rafa Benitez, Peggy and Paul Flanagan, at Melwood as Rafa hands over his donation.

Peggy, Warren Bradley and Winnie.

Lily.

never stopped her achieving the heights that she did in receiving her splendid spirit from the veins of Peggy and Winnie. She passed on a wonderful gift which will go on to last forever.

That is why there is a need for those who are more fortunate in health and wealth and even for those who are not to recognise that by just changing some established views and attitudes in the way that they see life; even if these small changes make them feel a little fearful or apprehensive, they can eventually arrive into a more meaningful and helpful world, one which will provide them with a warm and genuine sense of satisfaction.

Charles Dickens, one of the greatest writers and communicators of his time once proved the point in his novel, *A Christmas Carol*.

Ebenezer Scrooge, the miser who was enjoying enormous wealth and prosperity was driven by greed and avarice. His material world was built around money and possessions and no opportunity to make more would be missed. But no one liked him. In fact people feared him, he had no friends. No wonder!

Then everything changed when at a time of celebrations for all to enjoy he was visited by the spirit of an old colleague long since passed. Jacob Marley frightened the life out of him to make him understand his greed and decadent existence.

Fearful of what might happen to him he began to visit the home of the Cratchits. Bob Cratchit was his employee, his clerk and had been the victim of some appalling abuse in the past from the miser.

It was only then that Scrooge became aware of the Cratchit's plight whilst struggling to sustain a very sick child, Tiny Tim. It was this little child and his illness which inspired Scrooge to realise the error of his ways and once he had turned the corner, looked in the mirror an amazing change in his personality took place.

With this new hope, new inspiration and this new feeling of self worth he went on to become one of the major benefactors in his community, thus being able to provide a genuine account of his life on earth when it came to the time to make peace with his maker.

No one would attempt to suggest that there are many as bad as Ebenezer Scrooge was. Nevertheless the point that Charles Dickens makes is that even a little change of view, attitude or behaviour towards the sick and less fortunate can reap wonderful rewards.

The Giver

All I have is yours for you are all I have.

The Taker

It's so easy to break a heart. Those who live in a world without love cannot see this.

In their world there is no trust, no hope, no understanding only a greed for worldly goods, a lust for gold and a life that's so demanding.

The Giver

Walk with me through this world and I will show you generosity that you can never have imagined.

Of my love there is no charge, for it is without condition and you will learn on this journey that heaven has a place for those who care.

When it comes to the end of the road I promise you that you will feel better and more fulfilled.

All I ask is that you walk with me through this world.

CHAPTER FIFTEEN

WHO CARES FOR THE CARER?

To understand the magnitude of just how much Peggy and Winnie have given from their own lives to others in terms of care and support we need to have a general idea of what it is like to be a carer and a giver from a mere mortals point of view.

There are many givers amongst the wider audience who struggle on a day to day basis providing voluntary services for people in need of them, but gaining a valuable inspiration from the activities of these two women thus enabling them with the strength and willpower to carry on.

If you invest some time in talking to people who provide care for others asking relevant questions on how they see their roles and what support services are available to them some shocking and disturbing facts can be identified.

I have put together a few basic questions which I always ask fellow carers during our conversations and the same answers always dominate the response:

Q.   How much do you get paid for your care work?
A.   Nothing.

Q.   Why do you do it?
A.   Because I love him/her/them.

Q.   What other support is available to you so you can do the job effectively?
A.   I don't know. It's something I have never really thought about.

Q. You will clearly, at some stage feel the pressure which you are subjected to. Who can you ring or call on for help when this happens?
A. No one in particular springs to mind.

Q. Where do you find the time to look after yourself?
A. I don't really know, it just seems to happen naturally.

Q. Are you looking after yourself?
A. No, not really but what else can you do.

Q. Are you aware of any professional organisations that can help you?
A. No.

Q. If you were made aware of any professional or Government funded organisations who could offer you some support would you accept this assistance?
A. Yes, no question about it but I don't think that they exist.

Q. What do you feel would help to make your life a bit easier?
A. Just a little bit of support, no matter where it comes from.

Q. Why do you feel that people in general fail to recognise the work of carers?
A. I don't know really, perhaps it's because they have never had to do it themselves.

Anyone can do anything with statistics and figures but these are genuine answers to genuine questions given on a voluntary basis by people who are working within a volunteer service.

The objective here is not to apply blame to any particular body, public, private or otherwise, but to bring focus to the plight of carers in the way that they are viewed by society as a whole.

If unpaid carers decided to walk away from what they do on a daily basis our world would change at a pace that we could not imagine. The work that they do is so important in underpinning the NHS and the various affiliated trusts that if they were removed for whatever reason the National Health Service itself would be in danger of freefall.

So why do we as a nation disregard them in such a way that they become low priority within the corridors of power?

Perhaps the answer lies somewhere in the fact that care workers are not vote-catchers, so consequently, regardless of their obvious importance to society their work is devalued and unrecognised because they show little resistance in the face of corporate abuse and ignorance.

So how do we as a nation define carers?

Are they:

- Young mothers or fathers who look after the kids

- Parents of older vulnerable or sick offspring, who once in adult age are unable to look after themselves.

- Families and friends of relations and neighbours who spend time ensuring the welfare of their ailing charges.

- People who show a duty of care to anyone around them; displaying a natural responsibility for the community as a whole.

- Those who have been fortunate to do well in life, but feel an obligation to put something back into what they believe in.

- Professionals who regard their work as a vocation and are genuine in their motives but at the end of the day get paid a salary for what they do.

Out of the previous questions asked and answers given some information may be gathered which can help us to understand and so therefore attempt to put right the obvious imbalances within the nations priorities. Even though we have little chance of changing things quickly on a national basis, we may however achieve some success on a local community level.
So let's have a go.
What defines a carer?
What defines a non-carer?

Well, a carer of anything or anyone clearly gives things; money, time, prayer, support, goodwill towards whatever it is or whoever it is that they care about.

On the other hand a 'non-carer' may be defined as someone who is not interested in giving anything at all to anyone or anything, except perhaps themselves of course.

So, if the above definitions are looked at as logical we can break down into two divisions: The Giver and The Taker.

The Giver

All I have is yours for you are all I have. Please accept this gift of love as a token of my affection.

There are those who give who will never be able to understand why they give or even recognise what they give because they act out of instinct, it just comes naturally.

Others will consider carefully what they are giving towards and why they are giving it, and rightly so.

Some people will give to create an impression of how fine an upstanding citizen they are, which makes them feel important and although their contributions are welcome they are devalued by those who are aware of the truth.

Many of us give because we care. We may have a pet project which we like to contribute towards, or a particular charity which is close to our hearts. So, whatever the reason we give, whatever our motives, the outcome of our giving is positive.

Our contributions will go on to provide improvements to those around us, and the feeling of self worth within us through our giving makes it worthwhile.

The principle of 'The widow's pennies' also comes into consideration when we look at the true value of giving. Her four pennies were given with love and affection for the cause which she supported and so had a spiritual value which stood alongside even the largest donation given by the wealthy and affluent. So, although her gift may not be worth much in material value, the motives behind it were rich and precious.

Those of us who have grown up, eventually come to realise that money isn't everything. It is clearly important but it is far from being everything.

The home help who spends many hours over and above her call of duty doesn't do it for money. She does it because she cares for her charges.

The local lads who run the kids' football teams are not wealthy by any stretch of the imagination. They don't get paid; they do it because they love the kids.

Young people, and some not so young, who train to be fit enough for entry into marathons and other events, and then attract sponsors give their time and effort because they want to. It makes them feel better and they create something from nothing.

Taxi drivers who give up a days work in order to transport handicapped kids to the seaside don't do it for recognition; they do it because they care about the kids.

The list goes on and on. So it goes to show that giving is not just about money, it is about much, much more than that.

Those who give time, love, care, understanding and commitment are usually people who are in fact on low incomes; they do not have loads of money to give. What they do give though, is a valuable collective and substantial donation towards the improvement and quality of the lives of the people who genuinely need their help.

The Taker

It's so easy to break a heart. How can you hurt someone so close to you? Takers may be defined in different categories. Some takers are genuine and needy and deserve the benefits of giving due to their personal situation, which through no fault of their own have left them in a situation which makes them vulnerable and unable to cope with the everyday challenges that life throws up.

These are the takers that most givers aim their attentions towards, and clearly that should be the case.

But then there are the other takers. Those people who stride through life with a completely different attitude and point of view. One that is appalling to ordinary people.

The people who see worldly goods and possessions as the be all and end all of existence, they have no perception of how good it can feel to give.

The takers that we now discuss are those who can only think of themselves. They do not have the mental capacity to think of others, which then deprives them of a pleasure and wealth of feeling which can only be experienced by a giver, once a gift or present has been delivered.

In reality then, these are the real poor for they are incapable of enjoying the feelings of a giver. For them, it is impossible to think that they could be wrong. The sum total of their thinking is: 'what do I get out of it', meaning, of course, all things material. There is no inclination to feel a spiritual sense; for them this does not exist.

This type of taker will go to any lengths to take off anyone, regardless of circumstances. They will even take from each other if they can. Thankfully they don't get away with this behaviour for too long and once noticed people tend to avoid them. Shallow characters such as these with a narrow view of the world come from all walks of life and they are identified quite quickly within a close knit community like Scotland Road.

As well as being ignored they can be derided and poked fun at by their neighbours. Some of the quips I have heard follow:

'He's that tight there are padlocks on his bin lids.'

'He wouldn't give you a slide if he owned Switzerland.'

'When they moved house they took the wallpaper with them'.

'She would take the pennies off a dead man's eyes'.

So it can't be much fun being this type of taker. The one's I have met always seem to be unhappy, worrying about all their possessions all the time.

Especially so if they live in area such as inner city

Liverpool; where the natives are not backward in coming forward, with their taunts and derision.

Many people around these parts believe that life can be like a Christmas club; you have to put into it, before you can take anything out. And it follows that there is a lot of genuine admiration for those who look to be succeeding, provided that the success is earned 'fairly and squarely'.

It's the ones that want to keep the rewards of the Christmas club without putting anything in who are the ones that people have no time for. Whatever way it is looked at, the one conclusion that explains the actions of these takers is: They just don't really care.

Let's not give up on them completely though, for it has to be remembered that Scrooge was a boss taker, before he became a boss giver.

Finance

After the last fast car has been bought.

Once the largest mansion has been acquired.

After the most expensive magnum of champagne has been drunk.

Once the finest of cloths have been worn.

There will still be a need for tender care and attention.

CHAPTER SIXTEEN

LET THE COST OF THE FEW LAY LIGHT ON THE MANY

The Lily Centre is blessed in that it can rely on good housekeeping as well as diligent bookkeeping. Any potential giver can feel confident that their donation ends up exactly where they want it to go because all other expenditure is kept to an absolute minimum.

Prudence was of course gained from a very early age. Imagine how difficult it must have been to set up a project of such proportions as The Lily Centre now is, without any money. Only the total dedication, devotion and resilience of its pioneers supported by close family and friends enabled the idea to get off the ground.

Thankfully the local community recognised the work they were doing and so began to contribute towards their development, thus helping to broaden the scope of their services. Therefore it is fair to say that The Lily Centre has survived and flourished because of the efforts of the people to sustain it. People like its main sponsors, the Flanagan family whose initial and continuing support has been crucial in the birth and ongoing development of this phenomenon.

It has, in the main been their good financial and practical support as well as their morale boosting encouragement that has enabled Peggy and Winnie to drive the project forward into its tenth birthday year. "The more people we can get on board like the Flanagans, the more people we will be able to help." That's for sure.

Money makes the world go around and every penny

donated to The Lily Centre goes straight to the charity. There are no highly-paid Chief Executives, no merchant bankers earning fat pensions and no huge administration costs. Neither are there any large handouts from the government, just ordinary people working hard to sustain what they themselves created. In the words of Paul Flanagan, "The charity is close to all our hearts".

Even the local kids recognise the good work going on here, and turn up to the centre with their hard earned cash from sponsored swims, walks, silences and whatever other activities they can dream of to contribute. Every single penny that is collected helps The Lily Centre to survive.

Many of the supporters are not in a position to give cash but they donate time and experience which helps to keep costs at a minimum.

Pat Thompson, who donates both said, "I have been helping with the admin for about two years now, having been through quite a lot of trauma myself. I needed to do something useful and Peggy and Winnie, who are in my view icons, took me in like two older sisters would. They showed me how to smile again. They just don't realise the impact that they have upon other people".

The point Pat was making is very clear. The pleasure and benefit you can get by giving or being a giver can be immense and in Pat's case is very much deserved. Her contribution towards The Lily Centre is massive. Peggy and Winnie assure her of that and so she feels so much more 'worthwhile' in herself.

Pat's devotion is not just monetary; it is also physical commitment on a day to day basis. The sort of support she gives has saved The Lily Centre substantial amounts of money over the years.

Her story of course can be multiplied throughout the city. Dave Watson and Julian Flanagan must have felt the loneliness of the long distance runner as they completed the gruelling challenges of the Chicago and New York marathons in order to bring in much needed funds for the centre.

So here are just a few examples of the challenges laid down to the rest of us in what we do to sustain and develop the 'Peoples Charity'.

There is no point in discussing finance in the language of bankers on these pages. Better and more prudent to stick to what we know works. Good housekeeping, commitment, transparency and straight talking will always prove to be impressive to any would be giver and that is why there is confidence and optimism that many more people will 'get Lillied' in the future.

Once you 'get Lillied', and so feel the pleasure of being able to help then you will spread the Lily Centre message throughout your friends and relations. That's all we want.

CHAPTER SEVENTEEN

COMFORT ON THE WINGS OF A NIGHTINGALE

The future

So what of the future? Where do we go from here? Que Sera Sera. My mam once told me, "Look after today because tomorrow will look after itself".

Now that may be true in some cases, but not in others, depending upon what each individual has on their plate. In this case however, we consider the future on a much larger and important scale as it shall affect the lives of many thousands of people and their families who will come and go through the doors of The Lily Centre for many years to come.

Although nobody has a crystal ball to be able to know what to do for the best our activities and behaviour while we are still on the planet can have a huge effect on the ordinary people tomorrow.

In a hundred years from now people will read about the whole new dimension brought to the field of emotional healthcare by Peggy O'Brien and Winnie Keating just as we read in the history books of today about the work of Kitty Wilkinson and Florence Nightingale. By then of course there may likely be a cure for breast cancer as we know it, but equally, there will be other types of illness affecting the human race which will be challenging the people of the day. However, the brainchild of Peggy and Winnie will remain strong because of its unique original simplicity.

Genuine time, care and attention will always provide

comfort and warmth for people unfortunate enough to become sick, no matter what their condition may be. It will be quite a simple task to apply the values that these two women have pioneered towards many other ailments and conditions.

It just takes two, to make a dream come true.

Their work is already known worldwide and has so far been effective in India, America and Europe. The first ten years have seen the foundation stones being laid for the good citizens of tomorrow, in preparation for them to begin placing their predecessor's building blocks together to take forward this magnificent creation into their own world.

LILY OF THE VALLEY

I saw a flower
A beautiful flower
Blooming in the valley that is Scotland Road

It was a Lily
A Lily of the valley

I felt a warmth
A warm summer sun was shining down
Upon the flower giving life and vigour
Inviting it to breathe

I felt a breeze
Gentle and caressing, as it fans her silk like petals,
She softly blows her seeds
Onto the wind

Here I saw a beauty so special and unique,
So full of inspiration so strong
And yet so weak

Alas, she could not last forever,
As all flowers have to die,
She now lives in God's garden way up there in the sky

But then I see two angels planting in her field,
One is Peggy, one is Winnie
They are sowing Lily's seeds

With love and pure affection,
They tend to those in need
Bringing hope and aspirations to all of Lily's seeds

So now I see the future, of glorious green fields.
And Lilies growing everywhere,
Swaying on that gentle breeze

A lily's life, like every life is precious,
So high in all esteem
But close your eyes one moment
And picture in your dream
This flower's special angels
Sent from up above
Are sharing gifts amongst us

It's the gift of Lily's love.

Where is The Lily Centre

The centre is at 93-97 Silvester Street. Access by car is from Vauxhall Road, as all access roads from Scotland Road are blocked. If travelling by bus, the centre is facing St Anthony's Church on Scotland Road. There is a sign on the side of the flats indicating The Lily Centre and access to the block is from Woodstock Street into the car park, where our entrance door is also situated. We hope this simple map will help you find us.

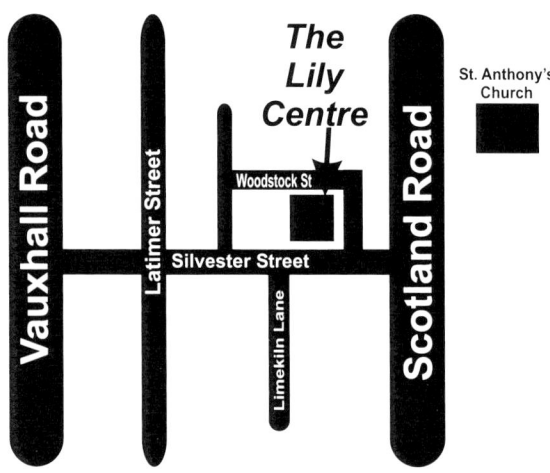

The Lily Centre
Breast Cancer Support Group

93-97 Silvester Street
Liverpool L5 8SF

Telephone / Fax 0151 207 1343 / 9055
Email lilycentre@btopenworld.com

www.lilycentre.org.uk

Registered Charity No. 1087847